PRAISE FOR
Sunday Morning Quarterback

"Insightful and clear-eyed."

—Richard Sandomir, *New York Times*

"[Simms] explains and lets the air out of some of the most popular made-for-television football clichés. What sets the book apart, however, are the many personal anecdotes Simms offers, in which he shares his unique perspective on key moments of great games and some of the NFL's most intriguing personalities, such as coaches Bill Parcells and Bill Belichick. . . . A good book from a great football mind."   —*Publishers Weekly*

"Might be the best football book I've read. . . . As fascinating as the anecdotes are, the best thing Simms does in this book is to trash a lot of commonly held nonsense about the game. . . . You're not going to put this book down, even for dinner."

—*Sun-Sentinel* (Fort Lauderdale, Florida)

"At times insightful . . . has many fun passages, mostly the telling anecdotes about the always interesting coach Bill Parcells."

—*Library Journal*

About the Author

PHIL SIMMS led the New York Giants to two Super Bowl championships and owns nineteen team records. After retiring in 1993 with fifteen NFL seasons under his belt, Simms has become part of CBS's top play-calling team. He lives in New Jersey.

VIC CARUCCI is the national editor for NFL.com. He has cowritten a number of books, including the bestseller *Do You Love Football?!* by Jon Gruden.

SUNDAY MORNING QUARTERBACK

Going Deep on the Strategies, Myths, and Mayhem of Football

PHIL SIMMS

WITH VIC CARUCCI

Harper

An Imprint of HarperCollins*Publishers*

A hardcover edition of this book was published in 2004 by HarperCollins Publishers.

SUNDAY MORNING QUARTERBACK. Copyright © 2004 by Phil Simms and Vic Carucci. All rights reserved. Printed in the United States of America. No part of this book may be used or reproduced in any manner whatsoever without written permission except in the case of brief quotations embodied in critical articles and reviews. For information address HarperCollins Publishers, 10 East 53rd Street, New York, NY 10022.

HarperCollins books may be purchased for educational, business, or sales promotional use. For information please write: Special Markets Department, HarperCollins Publishers, 10 East 53rd Street, New York, NY 10022.

FIRST HARPER paperback published 2005.

Designed by Elliott Beard

Library of Congress Cataloging-in-Publication Data is available upon request.

ISBN 0-06-073427-2
ISBN-10: 0-06-073431-0 (pbk.)
ISBN-13: 978-0-06-073431-2 (pbk.)

05 06 07 08 09 ❖/RRD 10 9 8 7 6 5 4 3 2 1

To Diana, Christopher, Deirdre, and Matthew.
Huddling with you has brought me a lifetime of
love, happiness, and tremendous pride.
—P.S.

To Dad and Dreamy.
Your love and support meant the world to me;
somewhere I know you're proudly kicking back to
read another one from your son and son-in-law.
—V.C.

CONTENTS

CONTENTS

SUNDAY
MORNING
QUARTERBACK

Sunday Morning or Monday Night, There's Never a Bad Time for Football

Each week, as I travel to NFL games for CBS, there are almost always going to be people who come up to talk to me about football. If I go out to dinner on a Friday night with our production crew and we're standing at the bar waiting for our table, I'll get all sorts of questions. I'll hear all sorts of thoughts and opinions. And at some point—usually after the second or third question or ten minutes into explaining why their team's quarterback should be benched, traded, or doing something else for a living, they suddenly stop.

"We're sorry," they'll say. "I'm sure you get tired about talking about football."

"You know what?" I'll tell them. "I don't. I really don't."

It's not merely an act of politeness on my part. I find the

game so intriguing that I don't ever get tired of talking about it. Anytime. Anyplace.

I get something out of those encounters with fans, too. They're a chance for me to do a mini-broadcast that can only help in the preparation for the real thing. For instance, if we're in Philadelphia and the Eagles are struggling—as they were at the beginning of the 2003 season—someone is bound to say, "You know, they should fire Andy Reid."

"No, they shouldn't," I'll say. "Let's think about it here for a second. He has taken you to two straight NFC championship games with a young quarterback. You have a tremendous defensive coordinator in Jim Johnson, who is working well with Andy Reid. It's only the first inning. The game's not over by a long shot, so be careful before jumping to conclusions. Nothing is ever as black and white as it might seem."

I don't know if I ever change anyone's mind, but a lot of times I'll hear, "Yeah, okay, maybe you're right." The frustrated talk becomes a little more rational, a little less emotional.

But when it comes to being a fan, we're all guilty of overreacting at one point or another. Even as an announcer and ex-player, even with all the information I get from studying videotape and talking with coaches and players, I'm quick to jump the gun sometimes because I'm a fan, too.

I never have to act excited when I'm talking about football, whether it's at a restaurant or on the air. My two most comfortable environments have always been playing sports and talking about sports. I grew up in Louisville with four brothers—Dominic, Tom, David, and Joe—and three sisters—Jeanne, Mary Ann, and Sara. Many times when we'd play pickup baseball—

which was a big deal when I was growing up—two of my sisters, Mary Ann and Sara, would be part of the game and hang right in there with all the boys.

The moment our broadcast crew gets to the stadium, I'm always enjoying it. It's always a good experience, regardless of how I might be feeling otherwise. You'd have to be practically in a coma not to find excitement in seeing that endless sea of red while taking in the delicious aroma of barbecue filling the air all around Arrowhead Stadium in Kansas City. Or while being surrounded by all those crazy, spike-wearing fans in Oakland's Black Hole. It brings back the same feelings of exhilaration I had as a player each time the New York Giants would go down to old RFK Stadium in Washington and we'd see all those overweight men wearing dresses and rubber hog noses.

I'm always curious to find out just how many of those detailed scenarios that coaches work on all week—when they're staying up until one in the morning just to take one more look at a piece of videotape that they are certain holds the key to success on Sunday—come true during the game. Having witnessed it from close range for fifteen NFL seasons, I can relate to the emotions, the thought process, all the hard work that some of these guys put into it. When you see a week's worth of preparation really pay off, it's moving, it's exciting.

I'm also anxious to see what happens with us. We've got exciting players. We've got coaches ready to call some exciting plays. We've got the prospect of an exciting game. Can we match it with our performance in the booth? Can I be on top of it well enough that, when something happens on the field, I can quickly and clearly explain to people what took place?

And then there's the excitement of just being on live TV for three hours. It's the one thing in life that allows me to actually stand up and say, "I know a little bit more about this than you do." That's a great feeling, too.

Maybe this doesn't say a lot about my life, but when I'm not doing an NFL broadcast, I'm watching endless hours of football on TV. If there are a hundred college games on a year, somehow I catch ninety of them—and that's on the low side. If we're doing a four o'clock NFL game, I'll watch as much of the early games as I can before we start our telecast. It drives the people I work with crazy when, as we're about fifteen minutes from going on the air and rehearsing our opening, I'll say, "Keep that game on! I'll watch it out of the corner of my eye."

I'll watch videotape of the games I can't see on Sunday. And I'll always watch *Monday Night Football*, even though it's on a competing network. For as long as I can remember I've planned my entire Monday schedule—work, play, eating dinner, whatever—so that everything is out of the way when *Monday Night Football* comes on and I can watch without being interrupted.

I'm tuning in to all these games for a lot of reasons, the first being just pure enjoyment. After that I'm making judgments and forming opinions. I'm judging the performance of the players. I'm judging the performance of the coaches, seeing if their teams line up properly and what ideas they have.

I'm also listening closely to what the announcers have to say. Just as, during my days as a player, I judged other quarterbacks when I watched them on TV or on film, I now judge other announcers. I judge them when they say things I know are not right. And I judge them when they say things that make sense—

things I wouldn't have thought of saying. This job is absolutely no different from playing in the sense that, as announcers, we're competing. I'm competing against the other networks. I'm competing against the guys I work with at CBS. I just think that's human nature. And that's the way I like it.

I don't kid myself about the significance of the announcers' role in the tremendous popularity of the games. The games sell themselves. I firmly believe that the ratings would be the same, regardless of who sits behind those microphones. I think I'm one of the biggest sports fans around. I watch a lot of sports on TV, but I have never—and I mean NEVER!—turned a TV on one, single time in my life only because I wanted to hear what a particular announcer had to say about the game.

But if you have any pride as a network, or as a person, you want to put the best product you possibly can on the air. Week after week, that's what we're trying to do.

Since the day it was announced that I was going to work for the first time as a game analyst, with NBC, the first question out of everyone's mouth was, "Do you think you can criticize the players?" I would say, "Yeah, I think so. I'm just going to talk about the game. If something I say comes out as criticism, so be it."

I've never thought, *Gee, I don't want to say that, because that's being a little too critical.* But I do have a great appreciation for the players and coaches. I know how hard this game is. When you talk about players and why they're struggling, you've got to have concrete evidence. You just don't go out there and mutter some words. When I express my thoughts, I've got to make sure they're clear, and base my opinions on strong facts. I owe it to the players, coaches, and, especially, the viewers to be truthful.

In the booth, I make a little sign for myself on an index card that says *Why,* and I put it over one of the monitors. It is not meant as a question. It is to remind me to tell viewers why certain things are happening in a game. Why are the Kansas City Chiefs running outside today? Why are the New York Jets having success throwing deep down the field when they usually throw short passes?

I can't just describe to viewers what they already can see. I am supposed to be the analyst. I am supposed to be able to explain not only *what* is going on but *why.*

CHAPTER ONE

"The Quarterback Threw into Double Coverage" and Other Observations Worth Tuning Out

"As Shakespeare once said,
'Even an idiot is a genius after the fact.'"

—Tom Moore,
Indianapolis Colts offensive coordinator

TV absolutely can lie. Invariably, when our production crew sits down for our first meeting before a game, one of the guys I work with will say, "Well, so-and-so was horrendous last week." That's an opinion based largely on what he saw while watching a broadcast tape of the game.

Let's say the quarterback was 10 for 24. That means the announcers who called the game most likely pointed out that the quarterback didn't have a good day because of those unimpressive statistics. Then, on *Sports Center* that night, the anchors said the same thing, only reinforcing an opinion forged several hours earlier.

But when we get together to watch the coaches' tape, that critical member of our crew is stunned to see that the guy he thought was "horrendous" actually played a much better game because he can see the whole picture. The coaches' tape provides an overhead view of each play from the sideline and end zone. For the most part, TV cameras only follow the ball and zoom in on the players throwing it, catching it, and running with it, and don't give you a true sense of what's going on everywhere else.

"Wow! Look at that!" our resident critic says. "He didn't have time to throw there."

Right away, you find out that you didn't realize the quarterback was under so much pressure, because TV didn't document it well enough. You realize it was, in fact, all because of the quarterback when he did make some completions. Under pressure, the guy's not open, and he makes the perfect throw. All of a sudden, of those 10 completions, 5 end up being great plays. Now your whole perception changes of what that quarterback did in the game.

You have to be careful with wide receivers, too. You might be watching a broadcast tape of a receiver who catches only two passes and your first conclusion is that he isn't doing a good enough job of getting open. Then you watch the coaches' film and see that he is getting open, but the quarterback's not seeing him or is not getting the time to find him or is not making good throws.

I believe it is every bit as important to prepare to broadcast a game as it was to prepare to play in one. A broadcaster who goes into a game unsure about the topics he is going to address would almost be like a quarterback who goes into a game unsure about the plays he's going to call. My gosh! I couldn't sleep if that happened. It would drive me crazy. If I didn't prepare for a broadcast it would be on my mind the whole time that my new partner, Jim Nantz, and I were standing in that announcers' booth on Sunday afternoon. The viewers depend on me to get it right. And I know what it means to the players, the coaches, their families, their lives, for me to be as accurate and as truthful as I can. Like it or not, what I say and what my fellow broadcasters say during a game can affect careers one way or another.

You always can tell if the announcers had or even took the time to study and get thoroughly prepared for a game. Many times they will make observations or blanket statements as if they were indisputable facts, even when they aren't. So many times when I'm doing games I'll make a statement, and when we run the replay, I'll say, "Uh-oh, that's not what happened." The replay gives me a view where I see that I was wrong. A lot goes on out there and you can't see it all, but when you're wrong you should correct yourself as you see the play a second or third time. What choice do you have? There's visual evidence that says you're a liar, so you might as well go ahead and say, "Yeah, okay, I was wrong." And you just move on.

Sometimes when you're broadcasting a game it's hard to admit you've made a mistake. I've listened to announcers insist that a play unfolded a particular way, even when the replay will show something completely different, but that doesn't matter. They're going to stick with their story. It happens all the time.

If all of this sounds a little pompous, so be it. I'm like everyone else: I think my opinion is the only one in the world that counts. That's why I doubt I'll ever sit in the booth with another ex-NFL quarterback—because we all think that we know it all. I'm sure other announcers listen to me and hate a lot of stuff I say. That's fine.

But for everything we say, there are consequences. I'm reminded of it every time people come up to me and say something about a football team or a player, and I'll say, "That is not true. Why would you think that is true?"

Almost without fail, the answer is, "Because I heard it on TV. . . . Because I read it in the paper. . . . Because I read it on the Internet."

"Just because you heard something on TV or on the radio or read it in the paper or on the Internet doesn't make it true."

"Well, how else will I know? I have to believe what I read and what people tell me in the media."

With that in mind, I've come up with a list of examples of blanket statements and clichés that announcers and writers have thrown out there so often through the years that they are accepted as gospel when, in fact, they often have nothing to do with reality. Here we go:

"The offense is too predictable."

One of my all-time favorites. It's almost never true, but I can't think of a time when it has been less accurate because there is hardly anything predictable these days about even the most predictable teams in the National Football League.

I cringe when I hear it from announcers, writers, fans—or even a blood relative. Once after a game I played for the Giants, my older brother, Dominic, said to me, "You know I could call the plays from the stands." I love my brother, but I couldn't hide the sarcasm when I said, "Hey, it's either got to be a run or a pass. If it's third-and-ten, it's not a big secret. We're most likely going to throw the football."

Most people who say offenses are too predictable do so because they don't think their team's offense is jazzy enough. If you watch television highlights of NFL games on Sunday you see a lot of unique things. Fans suddenly find another reason to hate their team because they're wondering, *Why aren't we doing that?*

You know what? Fans of the other teams are saying the same thing. But when you're watching the highlights of football games, you're seeing just that—the highlights. You're missing all the runs that go up the middle and don't get a yard. You're missing all the incomplete passes. You're missing all the times your defense doesn't do a very good job. You only see the exciting plays.

I get mad at myself all the time for catching the "highlight disease"—misjudging teams, players and coaches—because I watch highlights, too, and I start getting the same thoughts that everybody else does. Remember, one team's highlights are another team's lowlights, and many times I'll find myself focusing too much on those plays. Later, when I start watching game film and actually see the team play the full game, I realize just how inaccurate those initial thoughts were. I say to myself, *What was I thinking?* But I fell in the same trap that a lot of fans fall into.

One good example was when the New England Patriots faced the Miami Dolphins in a crucial AFC East showdown late in the 2003 season. The game was in Foxboro, which had just been hit with more than two feet of snow—very un-Dolphin-like weather, to say the least. The Patriots sacked Jay Fiedler five times. Tedy Bruschi sealed a 12-0 win and play-off berth for New England by returning an interception for a touchdown, which the crowd celebrated by flinging literally thousands of snowballs into the air at the same time.

After watching the highlights on TV, my first thought was exactly what I'm sure a lot of other people were thinking: *The Dolphins just don't have it.* But when I saw the coaches' tape, all my preconceived notions about the Dolphins went out the window. They had played extremely hard. They showed tremendous toughness. The game turned on one or two exceptional defensive plays by New England. After seeing that tape, I realized the Dolphins were so close to being in the play-offs themselves. It underscored the point of how a couple of plays can turn around an entire season.

If you don't hear, "The offense is too predictable," you'll hear, "They're trying too many gimmicks." I'll watch a game on TV and a team runs a reverse, which is a must in football today because teams have got to do anything they can to make a defense react to what they're doing instead of just allowing it to attack with little or no concern over giving up a big play. They've got to give it a reason to slow down because there is speed on every single defense.

But after a team runs a reverse that results in a loss or produces minimal yards, I'll hear the announcer say, "They didn't need to do that." Even though sometimes the reverse doesn't gain many yards, there's no way to document all the residual effects that the reverse has: It slows the defense down. It makes defenders start to think a little more and be a little less aggressive. As a result, the running play that might have gained only one yard before the reverse could now go for five, because those defenders hesitate just a bit in case they see that reverse again.

You can't document that simply by watching the game as an announcer or as a fan. Coaches can, because in studying the video, they look for specific instances when they were able to slow down the defense through play calling. That's another reason why you have to be careful in making judgments, especially when it comes to calling plays. Coaches don't call reverses just to be whimsical. They're calling them for extremely calculated reasons that they have spent an unbelievable amount of time figuring out.

There are a few things you can always second-guess. Tom Moore, the Indianapolis Colts' offensive coordinator, nailed it for all of us when he told me, in that booming voice of his, "As Shakespeare once said, 'Even an idiot is a genius after the fact.'" I've second-guessed game management and sometimes decisions on fourth down. But if it's third-and-10 on the final drive, with the game on the line, you have everything you could want in terms of tension and drama, and the offense runs the ball for no yards or 20 yards, this is what I'm going to tell the audience: "Man, that took some guts to call that play. When you call it, you're opening yourself up to be second-guessed. But as a coach, you knew that that was the play that gave you the best chance to succeed in that situation—and you've got to have the courage to call it."

We had a situation like that during the 2003 season in Washington: A little more than a minute left on the clock. The Patriots trail the Redskins by three points. They have a third-and-5 from the Washington 40. They run a draw . . . and get 2 yards. Fourth-and-3. Incomplete pass. Game over.

"The call doesn't bother me at all, because I knew they were trying to catch the Redskins' defense off guard," I said on the air about that draw. "It could have gone for twenty yards as easily as it went for no gain."

I wasn't going to second-guess it, because I knew what they were trying to do. That is the unexpected play for that situation, and sometimes it doesn't work. But sure enough, that night I was a telephone guest on a radio show and this was the very first question I heard: "Tell us, Phil, what did you think about that call late in the Redskins' game?" And I told the host, just because it only gained a couple of yards and the Patriots lost the game did not make it a bad call. If it had gained 20 yards, that wouldn't have made it a better call. Either way, I would have thought it was appropriate for the situation. That is one of the reasons why I am not a big second-guesser of play calling, because most of the time I think I understand what the coach is trying to do.

No, let me rephrase that—after all the film I've watched, I'm fairly certain I know what the coach is trying to do.

A running play that doesn't work in a tight situation really bothers fans and the media. An incomplete pass is one thing; at least you gave yourself a chance by being aggressive. When you run it and it fails, the typical outcry is that you didn't even give yourself a chance, because you're perceived as conservative.

Coaches think that way, too, sometimes. Andy Reid once told me, "You know, we could throw on first down, and if it's incomplete and it's second-and-ten, it doesn't even bother me. But if we run and don't get any yards and it's second-and-ten, that really, really irks me."

Even if a draw play on third-and-10 should get 20 yards, you won't hear me gushing, "Ah, what a tremendous call!" because I know it just as easily could have gone for a lot less. The important point is that the coach had the courage to call it.

"They've got to win the turnover battle."

Really? We sit around, studying and thinking about a game all week, and this is the best we can come up with? We need to tell viewers something they don't know. Specifically, we need to tell them why teams win the turnover battle.

You win the turnover battle because your pass rushers are making the quarterback throw off target and not see as well. That almost always results in interceptions. You get fumbles because your defense is kicking the crap out of the offense and the offensive line. You're hitting the running back when he's not ready for it, so he gives up the ball, or you hit him so hard that it's physically impossible for him to hold on to the ball.

You never hear that. What you hear is, "They lost the game because they lost the turnover battle." It says nothing.

Coaches talk about the importance of winning the turnover battle all the time, but they're not going to sit down and explain all the reasons why it is important because they don't have the time. But as announcers, we should explain it. Teams that win the turnover battle usually are the teams that are winning the physical battle. They're outhitting the other team. They're dominating the line of scrimmage. They've got the score in their favor. Now, scenarios change for the other side. As an offense on the short end of the score, they become much more predictable. The defense knows they're going to pass. Its chances of getting to the quarterback go up dramatically. Its chances of hitting him before he's ready to throw go up dramatically. All of a sudden, the defense gets turnovers.

If I had to cite the one factor that determines the winner in the National Football League, it would be the team that is winning the physical battle. It's funny, I start out every year forgetting this, and then somewhere during the season I say, *When am I going to remember this quicker?* As an old coach of mine once said, "It just comes down to which team's big guys are going to beat up the other team's big guys to give the small guys a chance to have success." In the long run, the winner of that little tug-of-war always determines not only who's going to the play-offs, but who's going to have success in them as well.

As much as we all like to talk about what wins and loses in football, how much the game has changed, how much time coaches invest in drawing up all those wonderful plays, it still just comes down to this: Which team is hitting the other one harder? Twenty years from now, that's still going to determine who is going to win football games.

Every once in a while you will physically dominate your opponent, yet still lose the game. You get some quirky plays, some crazy bounces, a couple of turnovers, a couple of calls that don't go your way. But over the course of a season the teams that win the physical battles will be far more successful than the teams that don't. I most likely don't alert viewers often enough about offensive line play and defensive line play, areas we all tend to take for granted but that have the most to do with deciding games.

As a player, I knew when my line was winning the physical battle without even having to think about it. The space I had in which to throw the football told me everything. If you asked me to go back and name the top 10 passing games in my career, every one of them would have one thing in common: As I went to throw the football I had space around me. That space gave me a chance to be a very accurate thrower. It also helped me see a lot better. The better I could see, the smarter I got in my decisions on where to go with the football.

When I set a Super Bowl record by going 22 of 25 in our victory over Denver, I only hit the ground twice the whole day—once while being pressured into an incomplete pass and the other time when I had a keeper late in the game for 22 yards.

Interceptions thrown by a quarterback almost always result from a lack of time. He can't get in position to throw because he's going to get hit or he simply doesn't have enough time to look at the secondary. I like to illustrate that point to people by holding in one hand a piece of paper with five words on it and covering the words with the other. I pull my hand away to show them the five words, and before they can even focus their eyes I cover them up again. Then I ask them to tell me what those words are. They say they don't know. I pull away my hand again, this time longer, and ask them to read the words, which of course they can do without any problem.

"That's what it's like for a quarterback," I say.

So many interceptions come because you just guess. With less time to make a decision, you become dumber. You think you see something, but maybe you don't. It's amazing how many unclear, what-ifs you deal with in a game. A lot of times you don't really know exactly what you did until you watch the film because the game is so fast and you're dealing with so many instincts and split-second decisions. Often all you're left with is a best guess. You get under a little pressure, you can't quite see, and then you throw the ball to where you thought you saw the top of a helmet that's the same color as yours. The pass is complete, the crowd roars, and you go, *Whew! Man!*

The next day as you're watching film, the coach says, "That's the way to hang in there and see down the field." You'd like to tell him the truth: "Coach, I really didn't see much. All I think I saw was the top of my receiver's helmet. I knew I was about to get hit, so I thought, *What the hell?* And I just threw it. And when he caught it, I was the most relieved person in the stadium."

I didn't have the courage to tell the truth. What I would end up saying is, "Thanks, Coach."

That stuff happens a lot more than anyone would care to admit.

When you're whipping the other team, of course you become very confident as a player and as an offensive unit. Cocky even. You just have that feeling that you're going to successfully execute every single play that's called. It does make you play better. An analogy that so many people can relate to better than being on a football field is playing golf. Some days you just have it. Even though you're only an average golfer, there's that day when you're hitting it better than the way you usually do. All of a sudden when you stand up to that ball, you're thinking, *Hey, I've already hit a lot of good shots. Why wouldn't I think I'm not going to hit another one this time?*

It was the same feeling for me, as a quarterback, and it had to be the same feeling for all our offensive players and for the person calling the plays. Now, we've instilled confidence that he can call a particular play and we'll execute it properly. It all snowballs and perpetuates itself. You're controlling situations. You're controlling the down and the distance, which determines your rate of success.

Let's also think about it from a defensive lineman's perspective. If an opponent is running the ball well on you, really ripping it up, what are you going to do? You're going to dig in a little harder, brace yourself a little more, because you're more determined not to get pushed around anymore. What does that do? It eliminates all possibilities of your being fast, quick, and reckless to get to the passer. So when the offense does run a play-action pass, it has more space, more time, more separation, because those defenders are digging in to try and stop the run. The quarterback's chances of hitting that pass have gone up tremendously.

I would always hear coaches and defensive players tell me there is nothing worse than the opponent running the football on you. It used to just go right over my head. I said, "Yeah, yeah, yeah, let's move on." But the more I listened to coaches and players and watched games, I realized that there was a lot of truth in that. Think of how demoralizing that is to the defensive players. They're giving up a lot of rushing yards, but it goes deeper than that. It's about your manhood. It's about what the game is about. How tough are you? How tough are we?

The harshest, most insulting comment you could have made to me when I was a player was, "Simms, you don't have the courage to stand in the pocket when the rush is getting close." That would crush me. And when you're the team that is running successfully, that's exactly what you're saying to that opposing defense. It's like someone spitting on you. It's like being slapped and pushed to the ground. It's degrading.

To give a good example, in 2003 the Cleveland Browns let Baltimore's Jamal Lewis run for an NFL-record 295 yards against them. The perception, and rightly so, was that the Browns' run defense was not very good (they would finish the year ranked twenty-third in the league against the run). We did their following game, against San Francisco, and I was worried. I thought, *Oh, my gosh! I hope they're not that bad, because this is going to be a really terrible game for TV if they are.* But when I watched the film it was a little different. Lewis ran the ball thirty times. Eighteen went for 3 yards or less—including six for no gain or losses—and there were some incredibly big runs mixed in.

When we arrived in San Francisco to prepare for the broadcast, I told the rest of the crew, "If you're the Cleveland Browns, you are so mad, you are so pissed off about what just happened to you, that there is going to be a reclamation project going on here Sunday." And there was. The Browns didn't shut the 49ers down completely, but they shut them down pretty damn well (75 total rushing yards, but only 32 by their running backs. Jeff Garcia, who ironically would end up as Cleveland's quarterback a year later, had 40 yards on scrambles), and the Browns ended up winning the game.

These are professional athletes, guys who have tremendous pride. These are coaches who have had their feelings and pride hurt just as much as the players. They were going to fix that situation, and they did. They ended up beating the 49ers, who were a heavy favorite.

But it would be wrong to say that the 49ers were caught by surprise. They knew the Browns were going to be mad as hell, and they had taken that into account. When you're a professional football team you almost don't want to see the team that you're going to play have such a bad game the week before, because you know they are going to pour all of their frustrations and emotions into trying to rectify the situation.

"When Priest Holmes carries the ball twenty or more times, the Kansas City Chiefs win 95 percent of those games."

I don't think there's a time that I hear this brought up on TV—whether it's about Priest Holmes or any other back—when I don't mutter to the person sitting next to me or to myself, "Ah, come on! It's not that simple. Do you really want to say just that? Explain it to me. Please!"

I'll give you a stat: If you turn on the TV any week during the football season it's a 100 percent certainty that some analyst is going to say, "When so-and-so carries the ball twenty times, that team wins 90-something percent of those games." It's about as meaningful as saying, "When Mike Tyson was at the height of his boxing career, he won every fight when he landed six straight uppercuts." No kidding.

You can't just mention a statistic like that, as if it actually explains everything. If you're going to say it, then give me the reasons why those numbers are what they are. The story isn't the statistic. The story is, why are they running the ball twenty or more times?

Here's why: Your offensive line is opening up holes for the runner, which allows him to have success. The game is close or you're ahead most of the time. You are controlling situations in the game, which allows you to still be patient, run the football, and keep the defense guessing. If you're leading late in the game, you're going to try to run out the clock, so of course you're going to get more rushing attempts. Also, your runner is probably pretty good, and that's another reason he gets more chances to carry the football.

What happens when the St. Louis Rams fall behind by 10 points, 13 points? They do what most teams do in that situation. They panic a little bit. They start to throw the ball more. They start worrying about the clock. They need more plays to catch up. And when they throw it more, they cannot hand the ball off to Marshall Faulk. Now if the Rams end up losing the game, you know the first thing you're going to hear out of a talk-show host's mouth literally seconds after the final gun will be: "They only ran Marshall Faulk six or seven times. When he carries the ball ten times or less, the Rams are one in nine. That's why they lost."

Mike Martz is a smart coach. He wants to hand the ball to his star running back, but the situation dictated that he could not do that. What would that same talk-show host say if the Rams were down, 28–0, late in the third quarter and they ran Marshall Faulk every time they had the ball? Hey, it's got to be a good idea, because when he gets over 25 carries, they have a great chance of winning the game. How absurd is that?

Many times numbers come down to what your team believes in. When I played for Bill Parcells, there were years when we believed in running the football, and when we threw it, we were looking for big plays. Bill wanted yards. I'll never forget one day in practice when we had a play-action pass called, and I had two deep routes that required high-effort throws. I looked, didn't like my chances of completing them, so I threw into the flat for a 3-yard gain to the back I had faked the handoff to. Bill wasn't happy.

"Throw it down the field!" he yelled.

"I thought the coverage was too tight," I said.

Then in a very sarcastic tone he said, "Well, what's the matter, Simms? Are we worried about our completion percentage and our quarterback rating? Is that why we're trying to get a completion to the back?"

It wasn't long before the sarcasm turned to anger.

"I don't need no quarterback worried about his stats," Bill growled. "I need big plays. We design them; this is what they're for. Don't be selfish worrying about your stats. Throw it down the field when we call these plays!"

The comeback I had in my mind—but was smart enough to keep to myself—was, "Okay. And when I go three-for-ten, I'm sure you'll take up for me in the paper, right, Bill?"

If you look at the 49ers from the start of the Bill Walsh era in 1979 all the way through George Seifert and Steve Mariucci, the system and the belief were that their offense was going to revolve around their quarterback. The result in the mid-1980s was tremendous numbers for their quarterbacks—Joe Montana, Steve Young, Jeff Garcia. Every time I'd look at the stat sheets posted in our locker room, Montana would be on top in every passing category.

Even when these quarterbacks got hurt, the players who came in to replace them put up big numbers as well. In 1986

Montana was out with a back injury and Jeff Kemp had taken over for him. One day I looked at those stat sheets, and I couldn't believe my eyes: Jeff Kemp, a career backup, was among the league leaders in passer rating and completion percentage. I thought, *You just can't get away from these 49er quarterbacks.* When Garcia was hurt in 2003 Tim Rattay was in there putting up impressive numbers. I don't mean to take away from the talent of the 49er quarterbacks, but sometimes the system and unwavering belief in it can influence and manipulate numbers more than the talent.

I didn't even realize that that was what Bill Walsh was trying to introduce me to when he came to Morehead State to work me out before the '79 draft. There was no combine then, so the coaches and scouts who wanted to see me came to Morehead. No one was advising me. I just took what I thought was a commonsense approach. I knew I would be timed in the 40-yard dash, so I practiced some 40s. I practiced throwing. I ran and lifted and got myself in the best possible shape so that I would look like a professional athlete. It is a big deal when those coaches and scouts lay their eyes on you for the very first time. They want to see someone they can envision wearing one of their uniforms. It's really the first test that you pass—or fail—and I was determined to pass with flying colors.

Bill showed up wearing a cream-colored sweatsuit that fit him perfectly. That silver hair of his was perfect. He was as cool as could be. As he watched me work out, he stood with his right arm across his chest, his right hand tucked under his left elbow, and his left index finger resting against his cheek, that same pose I saw a million times when he was coaching the 49ers.

Up to that point I had worked out for about nine teams, and every single person who came to Morehead wanted to see how hard I could throw. I was young, I had a strong arm, and I threw the ball pretty hard. In fact, when I asked Ray Perkins, the Giants' coach at the time, how he wanted me to throw the ball, he said, "Son, I want you to throw that ball as hard as you can every time."

"Even short passes?" I asked.

"I want you to knock 'em down."

Then Bill Walsh came along. I started working out, throwing hard as usual, and Bill said, "Oh, that's *waaay* too hard. Throw a little softer. Throw with a little more rhythm." I took a little off my passes, but again Bill said, "Oh, it's way too hard. Softer." Now I was thinking, *Okayyy.*

"I want you to drop back really gracefully," Bill said. "Be really light on your feet. And I want you to throw with beautiful rhythm. I want your passes to be really pretty. I want nice spirals."

After about ten minutes I finally got it. I finally got to a speed that he liked. For the next thirty minutes I threw just the way he wanted me to. My passes were at a nice pace, the perfect pace. They were easy for the receivers to catch. They were on time. I was throwing nothing but perfect spirals. As I got into it, I was thinking, *Hey, this is really cool. Man, this is great. This guy has been here fifteen minutes and I am like a machine.*

Of course, back then no one else was teaching that style. I had never done anything like this in my life. I had always been taught to throw it hard. Just drop back and rip it. But when you throw the ball hard, it gets away from you every now and then, or at times the receivers drop the ball. In about fifteen minutes to a half hour, I learned about the rhythm of throwing and being a little better technically. The results were awesome. That was one of the most enjoyable days I've ever had as a quarterback.

Bill came back to Morehead to work me out a second time. Afterward, he said, "Phil, if we draft you, you're going to lead the league in passing every year."

Before then I had pretty much been responding to everything he said with "yes sir, no sir" answers. When he said that I couldn't help but give him an incredulous look. Lead the league in passing? Every year? Even as a rookie?

"What, you don't believe me?" Bill said.

He proceeded to rattle off the names of other quarterbacks he had helped win passing titles—Greg Cook and Ken Anderson in Cincinnati (where he also helped Virgil Carter lead the NFL in completion percentage); Guy Benjamin and Steve Dils at Stanford, before they went on to NFL careers. We're not talking about history's greatest throwers, but nothing was getting in the way of Bill Walsh's quarterback having success.

The 49ers didn't have a first-round pick that year. They had the first pick of the second round, and Bill told me he was confident I would still be there. He was wrong. I wound up being a first-round pick of the Giants. The 49ers ended up drafting a pretty good quarterback on the third round—Joe Montana.

Joe didn't see much of the field as a rookie; he backed up veteran Steve DeBerg. Nevertheless, Bill stayed true to his promise of his quarterback putting up league-leading numbers. DeBerg ended up setting NFL single-season records for attempts (578) and completions (347).

• • •

A good modern-day example of designing an offense to allow the quarterback to excel is the overwhelming success that Kurt Warner had when Mike Martz was his offensive coordinator and then his head coach in St. Louis. The offense was absolutely going to gravitate toward the quarterback. The Rams were going to throw it a lot. Don't worry about situations in the game, whether you're ahead or behind, whether you're backed up against your own goal line or in the middle of the field. Keep throwing it. Don't worry about the interceptions. Throw another touchdown.

For a time that was how Mike Martz approached it—with no concern about the "dreaded" turnover. In fact, I know of at least one game that he entered with six 2-point-conversion passing plays. Six! Most teams only have one, because 2-point-conversion attempts don't happen all that often in the NFL. That tells you a lot about Martz's mentality when he comes to throwing the football.

The opposite of that would be what the Carolina Panthers did in 2003 with Jake Delhomme. He's not going to get a chance to throw it thirty to thirty-five times a game. The Panthers are going to run it, play defense, slow it down, nitpick. When they get a chance, they're going to try to score. Everything is just more cautious with the Panthers.

When John Fox left as the Giants' defensive coordinator to take over as the Panthers' coach in 2002 he was determined to play defense, play good special teams, and run the football. When they threw the ball, the goal was just to be efficient and opportunistic. By following that approach, the 1-and-15 team he took over in 2001 needed only two seasons to soar to 11 and 5, win 3 play-off games (2 on the road), make the Super Bowl, and end up only a few points and a few seconds short of being the latest NFL team to shock the nation.

It's the way the Tennessee Titans used to do it with Steve McNair. After the 1999 season, when they went to the Super Bowl against St. Louis, I did a Titans play-off game at Indianapolis. Somewhere late in the game, during a time-out, I asked the person who keeps statistics for us in the booth what Steve McNair's numbers were at that time. The guy handed them to me, and I was stunned. McNair was something like 11 for 17 for 110 yards. Maybe his numbers weren't even that good. I would have sworn that he had thrown for 250 yards or more, because every time he needed a completion, he would make it. Most of the throws he connected on were in crucial situations—third-and-4, third-and-5. He was playing great. It was spectacular stuff.

But if you didn't see the game and only learned what you knew from picking up the paper or watching highlights on TV, you would look at McNair's numbers and conclude that he wasn't much of a factor. Yet if you watched the game in person, you would realize that he played exceptionally well—that he was the kind of top-level quarterback people finally started to recognize around his seventh, eighth, ninth seasons; that he was the kind of quarterback who would share NFL co-MVP with Peyton Manning in 2003.

We'll be in a meeting before a broadcast, and one of the members of our production crew will say, "The reason this team isn't doing well is because Joe So-and-So's quarterback rating in the fourth quarter is 53.3." I'll lay my pencil down, sit back in my chair, take a deep breath, look at him, and say, "You're not serious, are you?"

Then I will try to calmly explain all of the reasons why I don't care about what someone's quarterback rating is in the fourth quarter. In fact, I don't want to hear it. I don't want to see it.

"If you put that on the screen during our game," I tell them, "I will call your name out loud on national TV and tell everybody what a stupid graphic that was that just came up on the screen."

We all get a good laugh out of it. I'm just having fun with the whole crew, but it does serve its purpose. My message is, "Let's not mislead the public if we can help it."

Here's another example of where you have to be careful with numbers: A defensive end could be having just a killer year, playing as well as he has ever played, but if he only has half the sacks that he had at the same time the season before, what is the conclusion we all draw? He's just not getting it done. Even though he is getting double-teamed, creating havoc, making the quarterback move out of the pocket, forcing the quarterback to make some inaccurate passes and some really bad decisions, we are still going to judge him on the decline in his sack total.

I say this all the time to people I work with, to fans I talk with, to just about anyone who cares to listen: The numbers in football lie; it's not baseball. Baseball is truly all about the numbers, and a lot of those numbers tell the truth. Baseball statistics can be revealing: batting averages, earned-run averages, on-base percentage. They all explain so much about what takes place on the diamond because the game is stationary and the environment is very controlled. In football, everything is a mess. Twenty-two people are running everywhere, so statistics cannot tell the complete story. Fans have to be careful when judging them and talking about them, as do writers and announcers—including yours truly.

"The reason they lost is because they didn't make any halftime adjustments."

When I hear people say that I always want to ask them, "Exactly what are those halftime adjustments you're talking about?" It's a thought and a phrase that's constantly thrown out there, even though it generally means nothing.

In fifteen years of playing, I can't remember even two adjustments we made at halftime. I'm sure we made some. All teams make some, but they're just never as significant as everyone paints them out to be on TV, such as blocking changes or pass-pattern changes or something drastic that's going to happen in the second half. You have spent a hundred hours in that week preparing for the game, drawing out detailed plans, and you have a contingency plan that basically covers almost every scenario in the game. Why would you need to make a lot of adjustments at halftime?

As a player, sure, I was part of conversations in the locker room at halftime that went something like this: "Hey, we called a couple of plays that didn't work. Let's not call them anymore and call some new ones." If that qualifies as an "adjustment," fine. But I just cannot recall making all those major changes that people in the media always talked about whenever we played a whole lot better in the second half than we did in the first. Either that, or maybe I just got hit in the head too many times to remember.

After our 1986 *Monday Night Football* game in San Francisco, a lot of people asked me what adjustments we made to account for climbing out of a 17–0 hole at halftime to beat the 49ers 21–17. I couldn't resist being a little sarcastic.

"What adjustment did I make?" I said. "Well, I tied my shoelaces tighter. How's that for an adjustment?"

I honestly can think of only one instance that I would truly describe as a halftime adjustment. It was in my last year. We went into halftime of a wildcard play-off game against the Minnesota Vikings, trailing by 7 points, and Dan Reeves got up on the board and drew up a run that he wanted to put in. I forgot what he called it, but he put it in, and I thought, *Okay, it's good. I can understand why you're doing it. But, damn, I wish it were a pass instead of just a sweep to the right from a different formation.*

Nevertheless, Coach Reeves knew, by running it from a particular formation, the defense was going to react a certain way and he had devised a way to block that defense. Sure enough, on our first series of the second half, the third or fourth play, we call that sweep, and Rodney Hampton goes around right end for a 51-yard touchdown. I almost want to say he didn't even get touched. I just ran off the field thinking, *That was really cool. We just put that play in and it worked for a touchdown.*

A halftime adjustment is really this simple: "We're running to the left; we can't get any yards. We're going to start running to the right more because we're blocking the guy over there better." Here's another example: "We can't throw against this guy. Phil, when you get a chance to pick right or left, go left, because the guy on the right is playing well." Or, "Let's throw it down the field more because they're doubling the wide receivers on all of the short routes."

It should also be pointed out that adjustments are made throughout the game—that if some plays are killing you in the first half, coaches will be trying to counter them immediately rather than wait until halftime.

Of course, there are times when you're simply getting your butt beat, and all the great thoughts and new ideas you might have are not going to change that.

"He's a real players' coach."

That is, perhaps, the worst label you could ever attach to a coach. It means he's soft, that he'll basically give in to anything the players want to do. It means being careful not to work the team too hard. It means being careful not to say too many negative things about his players because then they might not play as well for him.

All that rhetoric is great stuff for the working world—for people in offices with men and women of different ages. It's not conducive to being successful in the National Football League. You can't even think of having success in the NFL the same way you would in corporate America, because it's not a natural game. You are asking players to physically, mentally, and emotionally spend more energy than any natural human being wants to.

Who is going to get them to do that? Certainly not someone who says, "Oh, come on, son, let's see if we can get this done. I know you're trying your best." You've got to have a guy yelling, "Hey! Be quiet! Get in line! Get it done! And if you don't get done what I'm saying, we'll go find somebody who will do what I'm saying." You need a drill sergeant.

Fortunately, the league has some coaches who place heavy demands on their players and make harsh judgments and decisions without the slightest concern that they might hurt anyone's feelings. Bill Parcells is one. Dick Vermeil is another. I'm not going to list every one, but there are a lot who have that makeup, including a couple who recently returned to coaching—Dennis Green, in Arizona, and Tom Coughlin, with the Giants. They're successful because not only can they get their players to do all these unnatural things, but also their players don't hate them for it. The players know that to have a chance to win, they have to have someone behind them, pushing them, to drive them as far as they can possibly go.

I really didn't have any other type of coach, going all the way back to the one I had in grade school. Henderson Wilson, my coach at Southern High School in Louisville, was beyond tough. He was the toughest man ever to walk on earth. We practiced in full pads every day; he never heard of working out in just shoulder pads and shorts. Every day of my high school career we ran one mile before practice in full equipment, with the coaches timing us to make sure we were giving a full effort. It was your basic cross-country course, up and down hills, behind bleachers, past neighborhoods, to the finish line. On those rare occasions when he really felt soft, he would let us run with our helmets off. And on extremely rare occasions we would line up waiting for the whistle—and Coach Wilson would have enough mercy on us to say, "Take it to the field."

During the summer we would get on a bus and go scrimmage a team on the other side of the county. We'd get off the bus, carrying our shoulder pads and helmets. Coach Wilson would tell us, "Put your pads on. All right. See that telephone pole there and that tree in the distance? Run around the telephone pole, then around the tree and head back here." He would blow the whistle to start yet another mile-long jaunt. And this was *before* we even stretched for the scrimmage.

Wayne Chapman, who coached me at Morehead State, kind of looked like John Wayne, except he was probably a little bigger. But, man, he was every bit as tough. Coach Chapman was very similar to Bill Parcells in that you knew he had such a deep belief in what he was doing, you couldn't hate him for it and you couldn't help but buy into what he was saying.

While we were in Kansas City for the Chiefs' opening game of 2003, Trent Green, their quarterback, told me a story about a letter he had received in the mail during the off-season. It was from Dick Vermeil. The letter started out saying, "Great news. We have been selected to play in the Hall of Fame Game. That gives us one extra preseason game, and we get to go to training camp four days earlier. It's a good opportunity for us to get better."

Of course, as Trent pointed out, the players weren't quite as thrilled to receive the letter as Vermeil was to send it. The players knew that, by Vermeil's standards, those four extra days represented at least twice the amount of practice time for other teams. But Trent wasn't complaining. In fact, one of the qualities he likes best about Vermeil is the same quality that almost everyone who has ever played for him likes: that he honestly believes in his approach, and that he honestly believes he knows what is best for his players to succeed. All they have to do is follow his lead.

To get players to buy into that approach, coaches must have some success to show for it. That's the only way the players are going to believe in what they're being told. The coach can't just say, "Go hit your head on the wall twenty times," because the player is going to say, "How is that going to help me win?" Players need to see something that reinforces the value of what the coaches are telling them.

There are thousands of coaches who can take you out on the field and kick the hell out of you. But how many coaches can do that, make you understand why, and not have you hate them for putting you through so much hell? Not many.

Your football team is the same as a household. How do you want your players to act? To what degree do you hold them responsible for what they're doing? How much do you control the environment they're in? All of that influences how they learn, how tough they are, how they react to adversity—everything.

Bill Belichick has led the Patriots to two Super Bowl victories in three seasons, which pretty much speaks for itself when you talk about charting a course for success and never wavering from it. People often ask, "How can Bill Belichick be such a good coach now when he wasn't with the Cleveland Browns?" I'm not sure that it's necessarily true. He obviously learned something from his Cleveland experience and has corrected some of his mistakes. But the fact is, he had a team in 1994 that went to the play-offs, and they were widely seen as a play-off contender in 1995. The Browns got off to a strong start in '95, but when it was announced they would be moving to Baltimore, everything suddenly fell apart. Who's to say that Belichick couldn't have had the same success in Cleveland that he had in New England? We will never know.

There is a picture about Bill Belichick that has never left my mind, back when he was defensive coordinator for the Giants. I was getting ready to leave the stadium at about 7:30 one night. I walked to the back of our complex to pick up a videotape and heard this noise coming from one of the meeting rooms. I opened the door and there was Coach Belichick riding a stationary bike while watching film of the upcoming opponent. It captured him as a person. He was not going to take time away from preparation to exercise, so he found a way to do them simultaneously. He wore a rubber top so he would sweat more. He sweated so much on that stationary bike that it actually rusted to the point where one of the Giants' equipment guys eventually had to throw it away.

About a month later, at around the same time, I walked by that same meeting room and Belichick was riding one stationary bike and Al Groh, our linebackers' coach at the time and now the head football coach at the University of Virginia, was riding another. Both were watching film, talking and sweating up a storm. As bizarre a scene as that might have been, it told me how easy it was for another coach to recognize the benefits of Bill's crazy sense of multitasking.

You can't just talk about toughness. You have to teach it and apply it to everything you do in a football environment. I'm not saying this is the reason the Patriots won the Super Bowl, but I have to think Belichick's approach to practice, especially late in the season, went a long way toward creating an atmosphere that inspired his team to succeed. The Patriots have tremendous practice facilities, including a bubble, but you can count on one hand the number of times they used that bubble to avoid the elements. The temperature had to dip down to single digits, with winds blowing 30 mph plus before Belichick would ever concede that working inside was a better idea than working outside.

Bill Cowher didn't just luck his way into his current twelve-year run with the Pittsburgh Steelers, making him the NFL's longest-tenured active coach. But it is a pretty remarkable achievement, including the two-year contract extension he received in the summer of 2004. Besides that granite-like chin, his defining characteristic is a deep belief that being tough is the only way to succeed in the NFL. He believes in running the football at will. He believes in aggressive, physical defense that is as punishing as it is unpredictable. Teaching these principles doesn't take a lot of effort on Cowher's part, because they represent exactly what he is all about as a person and a coach—unrelenting toughness.

What do you see when you watch the Tennessee Titans? You see a team that always looks like it is in the middle of a street fight. At times they seem almost one step away from going outside the confines of the NFL rulebook, on the verge of total chaos. Is this an accident? I don't think so. The Titans are exactly like their coach, Jeff Fisher. They just love the action. Watching them reminds me of the warning I got as a kid: "If you pick a fight, make sure it's with somebody who is worried about losing; don't pick a fight with somebody who is just looking for action. Those are the scary ones." That's Jeff Fisher and the Titans. They're in it for the action.

Andy Reid is definitely a coach who, when you see him, you know he's a coach. It's funny. You just come across certain coaches that carry themselves in a way that they demand and command respect. You get that feeling when you're with Andy Reid. When you go down to watch the Philadelphia Eagles practice or do anything, there is no doubt who is the big kahuna on that campus.

Mike Tice practices the Vikings hard. You can see that there's a little bit of give and take between the players and coaches. But as I watch him talk to the players, during a game and during practice, I can see among the players that look that you have when you're talking to your father. You listen to what he is saying, you respect what he is saying, but there also is a little bit of fear because you recognize his power and authority.

I don't mean to be cold here, but being too nice to the players is almost always going to cost a coach his job. Generally speaking, a player will sell out his coach in a heartbeat. When things go wrong, the player will grab any opportunity he can, publicly or privately, to place blame squarely on the shoulders of the coach. *I'm just doing what the coach tells me. . . . Well, I can only run the plays that the coaches call.*

Check the local newspapers after a coach who was pretty tough on his players gets fired or decides to retire. Give it a couple of weeks, about a month, and you'll read all sorts of quotes from players saying, "He was too hard. . . . He didn't treat us like men. . . . We would have done the work; he didn't need to be so tough on us."

At the same time they can't say enough about how much they love the new guy because he "treats us like men" and he's "really a players' coach." That's the most condemning thing anyone can say about a head coach in the National Football League, because that means he listens to everything the players have to say. He kind of adheres to and goes by their whims, what they think, and he's definitely not tough enough on them.

Give those players a year, maybe two years, and this is what they'll say—anonymously, of course—about that players' coach they supposedly loved so much: "He's just not tough enough. . . . We don't work hard enough." This isn't something that happens occasionally. It always happens. It's guaranteed.

Go back and look at the quotes that were in all the New York papers in the aftermath of Bill Parcells's retirement after the 1990 season, following his second Super Bowl victory with the Giants. I'd say at least ten guys on our team spoke out, saying things like: "I didn't like the way he treated us. . . . He was mean. . . . He didn't treat us like men." On and on. Ask those same ten guys today how they feel about Bill, and they'll say, "He was right."

In 1991, Ray Handley became head coach of the Giants when he replaced Bill Parcells, who had entered the first of his two temporary retirements. I liked Ray a lot, and when he was one of our assistant coaches, I always thought he would make a terrific head football coach someday. But Ray made one big mistake. He thought players were professional enough to do the work without being yelled at or otherwise reprimanded on the field and in the classroom. He tried to treat us like men. He just assumed we were going to do our part, hold up our end of the bargain.

Of course, we didn't.

A comment I frequently heard in the locker room—and I

said it many times myself—was, "Coach doesn't have to be so hard on us. He doesn't have to work us so hard in practice every day. We can still get the job done without doing all this extra stuff." History tells us that that is just not true. After going 8 and 8, and 6 and 10, Ray Handley was fired. As one of my former high-profile teammates said to me, "Man, it was heaven with Ray as our coach. We just messed it up."

I don't know if there are any head coaches in the league who likes to have that "he's a real players' coach" label next to their name, because the connotation is that they're easy, that they're willing to bend rules, that they'll do whatever they can to be as accommodating as they can. Believe me, as someone who spent a lot of time in NFL locker rooms, you cannot trust the players. You have to push them and drive them to places they do not want to go, mentally as well as physically. It takes a hard-nosed coach to do the pushing and driving.

"The receiver's six foot three. The defensive back's five foot ten. Just throw it up there and the receiver will come down with it."

Sounds pretty simple, doesn't it? So why is it that we don't see very many teams throw the ball in that manner? Because even though coaches will do anything to give their team a better chance to win, they know the chances of successfully executing this play are not nearly as great as what we, as announcers and fans, might believe.

First of all, there are quite a few defensive backs who can play the ball tremendously well and can jump pretty high. They might even be better at jumping and reacting to the football than the wide receiver. Secondly, you're talking about the quarterback putting the ball within an inch or two of where the receiver can catch it. You're also talking about singling up one guy where height could be an advantage for the receiver, and those opportunities are few and far between.

Back in the mid-1980s we had a tight end on the Giants named Don Hasselbeck (whose son Matt is the quarterback for the Seattle Seahawks, and whose other son, Tim, is a backup quarterback for the Washington Redskins) whom we used to split out as a wide receiver all the time. Don was six foot seven— meaning he towered over most of the cornerbacks that played back then—so many times near the goal line we tried plays that had me throw the ball up where only he would have a chance to catch it. I don't remember once completing one of those for a touchdown because that short defensive back could react so fast and jump so high, he would always manage to get up in the air to knock the ball down.

Of course, it would be a different story if I were throwing to Randy Moss. But how many Randy Mosses are out there?

It's natural to assume that a big, tall receiver is always going to have a tremendous advantage over a smaller defensive back. However, the receiver quickly loses that edge if he can't get off the line of scrimmage because the little defensive back is much niftier and quicker and more athletic and just won't allow the receiver to get in the proper position to use his height. One thing comes with height, no matter how talented you are: You're going to be slower than many other players on the field who aren't as tall. The chances of a five-foot-ten guy being faster and quicker than a six-foot-three guy are great, especially in the NFL.

Still, as I was preparing to broadcast a 2003 game between the Vikings and Broncos, I discovered why so many analysts and others who follow football are so quick to assume that the taller receiver always will beat the smaller defensive back for a jump ball. It happened when I sat down to watch tapes of the Vikings and found myself saying, "Wow! Look at Randy Moss! That old 'just throw it up and let the big guy catch it' deal might just be true—for him." I could see Daunte Culpepper and Gus Frerotte lofting passes that, if I were still an NFL quarterback in the same situation, I wouldn't have thrown for anything. But they did because of Moss's six-foot-four frame and ability to consistently outjump defensive backs and come down with the football.

When I brought it up to Mike Tice, the Vikings' coach, in our production meeting before the game, he said, "Yeah, we have a term for it: It's called 'schoolyard.' When I say, 'schoolyard,' everybody knows what it means: just throw it up and let Randy go get it." If that isn't a sobering reminder of how a remarkably talented player can simplify this game that we all love to make so complicated, I don't know what is.

Mike Shanahan, the Denver coach, just started laughing in our production meeting.

"You know, Phil, it's incredible," Mike said. "They just throw the ball up and Moss catches it. Again and again. In all my years, I have never seen anything like it."

He proceeded to tell us a story that I actually retold during the telecast of the game: how in practice his scout-team quarterback, Danny Kanell, was instructed to scramble out of the pocket, stop, and just throw the ball as high and as far as he could throw it, à la Culpepper. What Coach Shanahan found fascinating was that the wide receivers who were not even his starters—and none of whom would ever be mistaken for Randy Moss—could adjust and catch the ball against his defensive backs at a high rate, even though the defensive backs knew exactly what the receivers were trying to do.

The more we talked about it, the more we realized that defenders are not used to seeing such long, arching passes, and they're not taught, as are wide receivers, to adjust to the ball while it's in the air. When you don't regularly practice defending against those kinds of throws, it becomes a very tough thing to do. Just from watching games and talking with defensive backs through the years, I can tell you that the longer and the higher the ball is thrown, the more time there is for the defensive back to look at the ball. The more time you're looking, the less time you're reacting. Anyone who has played sports knows what can go through your mind in a split second. A hundred things. The receiver has only one agenda: catch the ball. That alone gives him a big advantage. When that ball is hanging in the air forever and the defensive back is thinking too much and starts to panic, even more pluses go to the receiver's side.

Sometimes you begin to wonder if there isn't anything that the Vikings can't do with Moss. For instance, just before halftime of that game against Denver, Culpepper scrambled and just heaved the ball 44 yards down the middle of the field to Moss, who made the catch. As two defenders converged to bring Moss down at the 14-yard line, he made a no-look lateral over his right shoulder to running back Moe Williams, who then ran untouched into the end zone. The play was stunning. It was amazing. And it provided a huge momentum boost to the Vikings on the way to their 28–20 victory.

You don't see those jump-ball plays that often in the NFL because you don't see many receivers like Randy Moss. There are also very few NFL quarterbacks, such as Daunte Culpepper, who can launch it high enough and long enough to make those "schoolyard" plays work.

"West Coast offense."

When I hear people refer to the "West Coast offense," my eyes glaze over. The term itself doesn't bother me so much as the way people talk about it. I'm not sure what's worse—the erroneous presumption that West Coast offense has a universal definition or the equally erroneous presumption that it is some sort of cure-all, that it is the greatest thing out there, that it is the only thing out there, that it is unstoppable. Sometimes I feel as if I should genuflect when talking about the West Coast offense because so many people think it's the Holy Grail.

The roots of it do begin on the West Coast, with Sid Gillman, when he coached the San Diego Chargers in the American Football League in the 1960s. It even showed up on the East Coast back then, when the Giants had Fran Tarkenton as quarterback and Allie Sherman as head coach. It wasn't getting much recognition, because it was so different from what everyone else in the National Football League was doing. But Tarkenton was dinking and dunking, nickel and diming, completing passes and putting up numbers before it became a trademark of many NFL teams.

It was Bill Walsh who is credited with refining the West Coast offense and taking it to its highest level of growth and popularity when he coached the San Francisco 49ers. But nowadays, who knows what the West Coast offense really means? It has taken on so many derivatives. One version incorporates a lot of screen passes. Another includes reverses. Others call for it to be run from shotgun formation, something Bill Walsh never believed in.

The common thread in all versions is that everything is built around the quarterback's making completions, regardless of where those completions may be. If two receivers are open, one at 20 yards and one at 2, and you throw it to the guy at 2, that's okay. It's about the quarterback being the decision-maker, throwing in rhythm and being accurate. It's generally about throwing the football short and inside because that is much safer than throwing long and toward the sideline. Don't be concerned with down and distance as much as just continuing to complete the passes. Learn to pitch and catch. If it's second-and-long, either throw the safest pass in the world—like a quick screen—that's going to gain a few yards or run a draw that gets you back on track where it's third-and-reasonable and you can resume running your West Coast passing plays.

Yet it drives me crazy to hear people talk about it, especially when they try to suggest that it takes a special quarterback to run it because it involves a lot of short drops, precise timing, fairly quick decisions and throwing on rhythm. Who is this special quarterback? Give me a talented athlete or a good thrower of the football—I don't care who he is—and he will be able to run the West Coast offense. Everybody thinks the quarterback has to be someone like Joe Montana. Really? John Elway is not good enough to run the West Coast offense? Dan Marino couldn't have run the West Coast offense?

If you basically have good skills, if you can throw the ball and have decent size and decent foot movement at all—I'm just talking about average footwork—then you can run any offense in the NFL. Brett Favre's running the West Coast offense in Green Bay. I'm not sure that's the best offense for him, but he has done pretty well with it because he would be an outstanding quarterback with any offense.

In most cases teams aren't drafting quarterbacks who have been running the West Coast offense in college. These coaches are smart guys. They're going to gauge the skill of their players and do whatever they think will maximize that skill. It's not that difficult. If you have a 5-yard passing game, you want a quarterback who can do that. However, if you have a quarterback who can throw it 50 yards down the field with ease, don't you think you're going to try to get some of those passes into your offense, too? Of course you are.

I have to admit the West Coast is not my favorite offense. I prefer a little bit of a mixture of everything. I like to throw it down the field. I like play-action passes, especially in this day and age, when defenses are faster and tackle better. Also, it's much harder for receivers to catch short passes and get extra yards running than it was years ago because of the athletic ability of defenders. Everybody on defense is trained so much better on how to defend the pass. Players are taught so much more about it in high school and college, and it snowballs to the point where, when they become pros, they're very good at it—too good to give receivers the room to keep moving the chains after making those short catches.

Did I envy Joe Montana for the Hall of Fame career he had

and for all those unbelievable numbers he put up in Bill Walsh's West Coast offense? Yeah, there were certain parts of what he did and how he did it that I did envy. I remember watching a tape of the Falcons playing the 49ers, as I prepared for a game we were playing in Atlanta. It was Montana's third year and my third year. I just remember thinking, *Gosh! They're making it look so easy*. It was just one perfect-looking little play after another the whole day. Joe Montana is still, to this day, the most graceful guy I've ever seen play the position. He was perfect for Bill Walsh. That was poetry.

There were times when I would think, *Well, Joe doesn't know what it's like to get back and just try to stick it down the seam and rip it in there*. For Bill Walsh, that would be unforgivable. But for Bill Parcells, that was something you did quite a bit. We had our moments when we actually had a more prolific offense than the 49ers had. I think all quarterbacks always think about playing in an offense that is wide open. We all want and are jealous of the systems that are built for the quarterbacks to have success.

In 1991, my thirteenth season, Jim Fassel came to the Giants as quarterbacks coach and started teaching me some of the basic principles of the West Coast offense. I remember thinking I had heard a lot of the same things thirteen years earlier, when Walsh came to Morehead to work me out. At the time I didn't have a true understanding about what I was hearing and I let it go. With Jim—who would spend seven seasons as head coach of the Giants before becoming a senior consultant to the Ravens—I relearned some little techniques about throwing and body position.

One spring day during Jim's first year as an assistant coach with the Giants I was on the field working out on my own. I was just throwing 12-yard cuts to four of our receivers running patterns for me. Jim, who had been on the job for about a month, was standing there watching with Charlie Weis, who was our running backs coach at the time and who has since become the offensive coordinator for the Patriots. I was doing what Jim had taught me, and at one point I turned to Jim and said, "This is messed up."

Jim got this nervous look on his face.

"Why?" he said.

"Because I should have known this stuff thirteen years ago. I'd have been setting records in the NFL if I had known this thirteen years ago."

It was that big of a difference. It was unbelievable. In my last year, my fifteenth season, I was beat up, but I went to the Pro Bowl because I had learned with Jim for two years and I was starting to piece those lessons together well—how to hold the ball, how to relax, the proper steps to take, all the little things. Of course, I couldn't throw the ball anywhere near as hard as I could earlier in my career because I had had arm injuries and my feet hurt. However, in my fifteenth year, I could control the ball much better than I ever had in my career because of the techniques I had finally learned.

My first couple of years in the league, there was no such thing as throwing it too hard. Throwing back then was what I always referred to as just greed. If you had to get 20 yards, it was just, "Come on! Let's throw it to get twenty." It didn't matter what the pass was. I'd just throw it hard. That seemed to cure it all, but resulted in a tremendous amount of drops. Now, looking back, how stupid was that?

The fact is, not enough pro quarterbacks get detailed instruction today. There are coaches in the NFL teaching quarterbacks, but they basically teach you where to throw it. You'd better already know how. Teams are teaching more and more mechanics, but it's very tough. Throwing is such a unique thing. It's hard to teach.

I've said this to any number of head coaches in the league: "Wait. You teach your nose guard all these different techniques on how to defend a block and how to do this and that. And you're telling me you can't teach your quarterback techniques? The most important guy on your team? The guy who handles the ball every play?"

They'll say, "That's a good point."

Think of the throwing motion, all that's involved in it. A lot of a quarterback's talent is natural, of course, but you can refine the talent. As somebody once said to me, bring the sun one degree closer to the earth and it burns it up. It's the same with talented young quarterbacks. If you teach techniques that they can rely on and repeat, you get greatness. It's a fact in all sports.

The biggest bugaboo for NFL quarterbacks and all quarterbacks for that matter is they don't realize what it means to be committed to working on their techniques. It means an incredible amount of repetition. If you are a high school quarterback, you need to get a good idea about what your techniques should be and start working on them around March. You need to throw three to four days a week, casually or seriously—and at least twice a week seriously—for six months. If you get all of those repetitions in, you might be able to apply what you've learned when you go and practice with your team.

What do basketball players do in the off-season? They go shoot baskets all the time. What would be the difference between that and playing quarterback in the NFL? You're talking about developing a unique and refined feel with your hands. The main focus of a quarterback's job is to throw the football. Improving your overall strength and running ability will help make you a more complete player, but you cannot allow any other part of your training to take priority over throwing the football.

Before going out to conduct a quarterbacking clinic to high school coaches, I stopped by Giants Stadium and watched videotape of current NFL quarterbacks, looking for examples of the dos and don'ts of playing the position. Finding the don'ts was easy. As I searched for what today's NFL quarterbacks did well, it was amazing how many times I came back to Peyton Manning. He just did everything the right way.

I'm talking about his mechanics—the way he held the ball, his foot movement, and especially his foot placement. No matter where the receivers were on the field, he could maneuver his feet fast enough to get in a position to throw the football correctly. It didn't matter whether he was throwing short or throwing long, he always did it right. I actually had to struggle to avoid using him for every good example.

How did Peyton Manning reach that point? Natural talent is a large part of it, but equally important was the fact that he invested countless hours and countless repetitions. He worked on doing it the right way. He practiced perfectly. That lesson should be registering with more young quarterbacks, from high school to the NFL.

CHAPTER TWO

"Managing" the Game and Taking the Blame

"I think we just set a record for
the fastest game in NFL history."

—Wellington Mara, New York Giants owner

Some might consider calling a quarterback a "game manager" insulting, or at the very least, condescending. Basically, it says, "You really don't have a lot of talent, so everybody's got to do the work for you. Just make sure that you don't screw it up." It means that a football team is predicated on playing defense, being pretty good on special teams, running the football—and at the very bottom of the list is the quarterback's contribution.

If that's how you set up your team, if you'd rather not have all the focus on your quarterback, so be it. But here's something you should understand: It is absolutely one of the toughest jobs a quarterback can have.

I've had many discussions about this with Dan Marino, one of my CBS cohorts. We've talked quite a bit about football over the years, and we disagree on a lot of things. But believe it or not—and maybe it's because these conversations often have taken place after playing golf all day and having a couple of adult beverages—Dan actually agrees with me that strictly being a game manager is, by far, the hardest way to play quarterback.

Here's what I mean: A team that wants its quarterback to manage a game is mainly going to run the football. When you're a running team that automatically tells you as a quarterback that there are going to be a lot of third-down situations that you're going to be asked to convert. Even when you're running the offense well you will get third-and-3, and third-and-4 quite a bit. What's so hard about that? In the NFL those are obvious passing situations. That means you have to be very precise to make the completions to keep a drive going. You have to be a highly accurate passer to play that style because there's just no room for error.

As I mentioned to Marino, "Think about it, you knew going into a football game, regardless of how it was going, that you were probably going to throw the ball at least thirty times, most likely around thirty-five. So you were able to get into a rhythm, get comfortable, get a good feel of what was going on with the pass rush. And you had to know, as the game wore on, that the pass rushers would probably get tired because of all those times they were coming after you."

"You're right," he said.

"Now, how would you have felt if you had to go into a game knowing you were going to throw it between seventeen and twenty-two times when you can't get quite the same feeling, you can't get in the rhythm of throwing the football?"

Dan didn't have to answer that one. It's a tough way for a quarterback to go about his business. Yet even when those "game managers" thrive, you'll hear someone with a microphone say, "Well, they don't ask him to win the game. All he has to do is not lose it."

Sure, that's all they're asking him to do. And while he's at it, he just has to keep completing those high-precision throws. He just has to keep converting third downs. Oh, and by the way, he also has to make sure his team scores enough points to win the game. Besides that, they're not asking him to do much at all.

Give me a break.

One of the best examples of superb work by a so-called game manager in recent history is Trent Dilfer during the Baltimore Ravens' Super Bowl–winning season in 2000. Trent appeared in eleven games that year, averaging a little more than 20 pass attempts per game. He was probably in the toughest game-managing situations I've seen a quarterback have to face in quite a while. The Ravens ran the football with Jamal Lewis. They did have Shannon Sharpe at tight end, but they weren't as diverse as an offense as many of the other teams I've seen play that style.

As a result, the common perception that the media and public had of Trent Dilfer was that he was just not very good. I read that about him throughout that season, whether the games were good or bad—and there were some bad ones. I read that about him during the play-offs. And in the days leading up to Super Bowl XXXV, national writers were saying, "The Baltimore Ravens are going to the Super Bowl and might win it with the worst quarterback in history."

In history? That's pretty strong. The Ravens won the game, 34–7. Trent threw only 25 passes. He completed a dozen of them for all of 153 yards and a touchdown. But by no means do I think the Ravens got those Super Bowl rings with the help of the worst quarterback in history. Not by a long shot.

After that Super Bowl, I was in Kauai, Hawaii, as an analyst for CBS's taping of the annual *Quarterback Challenge,* a made-for-TV event in which quarterbacks throughout the league compete in a series of passing drills, with the winner decided by the highest point total. While Trent was on the field, going through a drill, I was standing on the sidelines with some of the other quarterbacks in the competition. A prominent quarterback in the NFL suddenly turned to me and asked, "So what's the deal with Trent Dilfer?"

"What do you mean?" I said.

"He should be a huge star. He's big. He's strong. He's a natural-born leader; you can see that when you're around him. And he can really throw the football."

I agreed. This was a classic case where perception, based on Dilfer's role in the Ravens' offense, was overshadowing the reality of what the player and the man were all about. And here was another quarterback, one of the best in the NFL, recognizing it. That was a huge compliment when you consider that most quarterbacks are particularly harsh in judging other quarterbacks because that's their competition, the people they're fighting against all the time.

Of course, that "game manager" label was slapped on me later in my career, especially in our second Super Bowl season in 1990. And that label was absolutely true. It was my twelfth season in the NFL, so I couldn't care less what you labeled me. I was past that. I took a lot of pride in being the game manager because I had had some success. I had won a Super Bowl. I had been a Super Bowl MVP. I had been to the Pro Bowl. All that mattered was winning games, and I knew that being a game manager was going to give the Giants the best chance to win. And, yes, I also knew that if I wanted to stay on the field, that was the kind of quarterback I had to be.

We became that style of team because we were extremely big up front. We were powerful. We had a big running back in O. J. Anderson. And we were just going to grind it out, 3 and 4 yards at a time, and slow the pace of the game. We were probably the first team to really overaccentuate managing football games. It was run the ball, milk the clock, play good defense, and win a low-scoring contest.

A quarterback is often asked to be a "game manager" because the coaches are convinced that's the best way to win the game. Most of the time they're right, but coaches have an easier time doing that when the quarterback is not a superstar. Guys like Dan Marino and John Elway were never asked to do that. Brett Favre and Drew Bledsoe have never been asked to do it, either. When you have quarterbacks of that caliber, you're just not going to say, "Manage the clock." You're going to take advantage of the rare talents they have throwing the ball. You don't ask a Thoroughbred horse capable of winning the Kentucky Derby to plow the field.

I've played in a wide-open offense and a very controlled, measured offense. Even though everybody perceived us as a running football team in 1986, we were a very explosive passing team. And even though the 1990 club was perceived as being "three yards and a cloud of dust," you go back to the statistics at the end of the year. Which team led the NFL in points scored on the opening drive? The New York Giants. Which team led the NFL in fewest points allowed on opening drives? The New York Giants. That tells you that at the start of almost every game we were in control of the scoreboard. Once we were in control of the scoreboard, our goals and agenda changed drastically. You just start playing percentages. If we were ahead 7–0, and there were 7 possessions left in a game, we would start slowing down the clock to reduce that possession total to 6 or even 5. Therefore, our chances of winning that game increased dramatically.

The offensive style we played on the '90 team was harder to run, because with fewer opportunities to make plays throwing the ball, our mistakes were more magnified. When you're a passing team, you throw it 35 to 40 times a game. So what if you throw an interception or two, miss a guy or two? You'll get it back the next play. That's not the case when you're throwing on a limited basis.

I've talked about this with a lot of top current and former quarterbacks. Everybody agrees that when you throw more, you get in more of a rhythm. You see better, you react better. It's like hitting golf balls. If you hit twenty, don't you get in a groove and doesn't it start getting easier? It's the same with the quarterback throwing the football. It's much easier to be grooved and methodical when you do it a lot.

In a controlled offense you have to resort to finding accomplishments that don't involve throwing the football to give you a feeling of satisfaction that you really did make a contribution to a win. In 1990 there were times when I came out of a game and thought, *I played pretty well. I drew the defense offside to give us a first down and three more plays—running plays! It took two and a half more minutes off the clock, which gave the other team one less opportunity.*

It's funny how you can get gratification from something that no one else but you, the coaches, and a few of your teammates would understand or even recognize. It's not easy for a quarterback, but you must be able to humble yourself to run this style of offense.

In practice during that '90 season, of course we put a lot of time into working on our running game. And because we ran so often and so well, when we did throw play-action passes, they usually were pretty effective. Another by-product of being a running team is that you face a lot of third-down situations, so we practiced quite a few of them as well. When you know you're going to be in a lot of those situations, it's amazing how many ways you can find to throw the ball 5 yards. The more we found, the more proficient we became at getting those first downs.

But playing that style can create tension with the fans and the players. If, on back-to-back series, you run two times and throw on third down without picking up a first down, boy, it makes you tight. It would make me nervous, really put me on edge. It wouldn't be long before you could hear the murmurs throughout Giants Stadium. When you throw the football a lot, it's easy to get emotion—from within the team as well as from the fans—and momentum on your side. In 1990, I would be happy when O. J. Anderson would get four yards on a carry. But a 4-yard carry doesn't get the crowd all that pumped up.

I will say this for those Giant fans back then: They knew that we were trying to control the tempo and pace of games, and got involved in it. A good example of that was when we played the Dolphins in the third game of the 1990 season on a windy day in Giants Stadium. On the second possession we held the ball for what seemed like forever. The seventeen-play drive covered 57 yards and, even though it resulted only in a field goal, we chewed up 10 minutes and 25 seconds. We converted a third-and-1 with a 1-yard run up the middle, and a fourth-and-1 and a 2-yard carry off right tackle. The crowd couldn't have reacted more enthusiastically if those had been 50- or 60-yard passes.

It wasn't until the start of the second quarter that Dan Marino took the field for the Dolphins' second drive . . . and a few minutes later we had the ball back. As I returned to the field for our third possession, Bill Parcells actually looked at me and said, "Work the clock." He was already formulating thoughts about how we were going to shorten the game. By shortening the game, that gave Dan 5, 6, maybe even 10 fewer throws than we would have had to deal with otherwise. Sure enough, the Dolphins didn't get the ball again until almost halfway into the second quarter.

Final time of possession: Giants 40:18, Dolphins 19:42. Final score: Giants 20, Dolphins 3.

Even now I can remember that Miami game very vividly and it makes me laugh. The great Dan Marino and that high-flying Dolphin offense never even got close to being a factor in the game. But I have to admit: I did a tremendous job of handing off the ball that day.

I remember walking into the locker room after the game, tearing tape off of my wrists, and I saw our owner, Wellington Mara. Mr. Mara looked at his watch, then looked at me and said, "I think we just set a record for the fastest game in NFL history." The game was only 2 hours and 46 minutes. Then Mr. Mara laughed and said, "The network sure has a lot of time to fill."

That didn't hit me at the time, but now that I'm in television I understand that you have a three-hour window for a game, and when you fall short of that you have to run a lot of filler—player interviews, you go back to the booth to ask the announcers to analyze the game one more time, you throw it back to the studio to show one or two more highlights. It's a challenge, but you have to get those commercials on the air. Of course, as I was tearing that tape off my wrists in the locker room, I was way too happy to think about any headaches we might have caused the people at the network.

Let me take this opportunity to pass along a belated apology. Yeah, right.

Let me also take this opportunity to say that we would go 10–0 that season, and 11–2 before I would suffer a broken left foot in a loss to Buffalo. Jim Kelly, the Bills's Hall of Fame quarterback, injured his knee in the same game. The next day, Jim gave me a call.

"Tough break for both of us," he said. "But I'll see you in the Super Bowl."

"Jim, I hope that's true," I said. "You might make it there, but I know I won't. I'm done for the season."

Fortunately, Jim was right about the Giants and the Bills facing each other in Super Bowl XXV, which we won after the most memorable fielf-goal miss in the history of the game.

Unfortunately, I was right, too.

And the list continues . . .

"Running is the added dimension that a quarterback brings to the table that other guys can't."

You hear people in the media talk about the mobility of quarterbacks as if it's the answer to everyone's football prayers. The first mistake is buying into the notion that throwing is equal across the board for all quarterbacks and that what separates them is the ability to run. That's absurd. For some reason fans (and some announcers) believe every quarterback has the same ability to read defenses, react to what he sees, shuffle in the pocket, and throw the football. They say, "To be different, you've got to run for three yards . . . you've got to run for seven yards . . . you've got to scramble . . . you've got to be exciting."

But not every quarterback has the same talent when it comes to throwing the ball. And when I talk about throwing the ball, I'm talking about all of the elements involved in a quarterback's successfully delivering a pass in the NFL—arm strength, accuracy, touch, throwing from different angles. I don't just mean the ability to cover a great distance. There are a lot of people who can rear back and throw it 60, 70, 80 yards. But can they throw out cuts? Can they change their touch? Can they manipulate the football the way they need to, throwing it sidearm if necessary?

There are tremendous degrees of separation in the throwing ability of NFL quarterbacks. Throwers are far more unique than runners because there are a lot more people who can run than throw. There are very few great throwers out there, yet when, after seeing a great pass on television, was the last time you heard someone say, "That's what he brings that other quarterbacks can't?"

Why don't we talk about the element that's missing with a running quarterback—that sometimes, when he runs, he ignores wide-open receivers? Maybe he gains 7 yards to get the first down, but he may gain 30 yards if he would just throw it to the open receiver. He doesn't see that receiver because he lacks the patience to stand in there and try to find the open man. When quarterbacks run too much, they are taking away some of the best, if not THE best, weapons on their team—receivers who have the chance to excel down the field with their own abilities.

Most people can't differentiate from a really good thrower in the NFL to an average one to a poor one, so they don't try. Even if they could tell the difference, I don't know if there's time to show it in a telecast. What they will say is, "Boy, I'll tell you, it's especially tough to play against this quarterback because he runs so well." And what is that quarterback doing? He's throwing for 130 yards, scrambling for 9, and his team is scoring 11 points a game. But, oh, yes, he does have that "added dimension."

I can see running becoming less and less prevalent with pro

quarterbacks because defenses adapt. The days of a quarterback thinking he's going to make it happen on his own with his legs are nearing an end, if they aren't over already. You've got to be a system-oriented, methodical quarterback able to move every once in a while when the system breaks down. That's the ultimate—running the system, doing what it asks you to do, taking advantage of the throwing opportunities, but also having the perfect instincts to know that when the pass isn't going to happen, it's time to run.

The extreme would be for Michael Vick, who in a short time with Atlanta established himself as one of the greatest runners the quarterback position has ever seen, to be a fairly patient pocket quarterback who takes advantage of passing opportunities, and then when he knows he has to run he's still able to make it work. But that's hard to do. It's inherent in any athlete's mind to think, *Why sit and wait? I'll just make it happen on my own.*

You've been trained to know that running can do good things for you, so it's just common sense that you're not going to be as patient looking for receivers down the field as somebody who doesn't have that great ability to run. The guys who stand in the pocket until the last possible second and take the hit as they throw are the guys that, athletically, don't have the option of running.

It would be stupid for Michael Vick to stand there and be that kind of quarterback. Still, you have to teach him and hope he matures to the point where you end up with the best of both worlds as a thrower and a runner. I've never seen a quarterback come into the league and get faster. All quarterbacks slow down. Even the ones who played that way for a long time, the Randall Cunninghams, reach a point where they can't do it anymore.

Vick is going to have his moments because he is part of an offense that, at times, is going to be much better than the defense it faces and he is going to be able to do his thing. But in most of the games he plays, when he runs, look out, because the players chasing him are getting faster every year . . . and every year, he's getting slower.

In general, defenses can definitely keep their eyes on the quarterback better than they have in the past. They're playing more zone coverages. They're learning they don't just have to guard a guy and turn their back to the rest of the offense. They're learning to cover people when they come into their areas.

A lot of that has to do with the style of defense the Tampa Bay Buccaneers started to play under Tony Dungy. Coaches around the league liked some of the principles the Bucs were teaching, so a lot of teams have tried to copy them. They're finding out that type of defense seriously limits the quarterback's mobility, because when the quarterback runs, defenders converge too fast. As you fake that first guy silly, three others are coming from the side, full speed, and you cannot avoid them. It's as with those velociraptors in *Jurassic Park,* where one of them gets in front of you, looks into your eyes to divert your attention, while others attack you from the sides.

You want your quarterback to be mobile, but mobility has to happen more behind the line of scrimmage and inside the pocket. By far, the safest place for a quarterback to move after he drops back is not right or left. It's almost always straight ahead, because the pass rushers are going up the field and you can see your passing lanes. When you step up in the pocket, you create space, time to throw, and running and throwing are both options.

Once you begin moving laterally you've limited your throwing options dramatically, except for a few guys who are so phenomenal physically that they can throw as well across their bodies as they can straight ahead. When you go sideways, you really can only throw the ball toward the sideline you're running to because it's hard to throw the ball straight down the field. In addition, defensive linemen get off their blocks because your offensive linemen don't know where you're going. You also find that, even though you're pretty fast, you can't outrun a lot of these super-fast, super-athletic defensive linemen.

Steve Young might be the best example in history of a quarterback who combined great scrambling and passing ability. As a young quarterback, if he couldn't find an open receiver right away, he immediately thought, *Run, run, run*. Then it got to the point where he said to himself, *Let's look. Let's run*. Then it was, *Let's look, look. Let's run*.

When did Young become just a dynamic quarterback? When he blended together reading defenses and throwing the football with his tremendous ability to run when he needed to. For the last four or five years of his career, Steve Young and that 49er offense were almost impossible to defense. Was it just a coincidence that he was able to develop all these skills and mesh them together when he started working with Bill Walsh in that quarterback-friendly scheme? I don't think so.

John Elway was almost the best of both worlds during his Hall of Fame career with Denver. He was big enough to take the punishment as a pocket passer. He was fast enough to be a mobile quarterback—although he mainly scrambled to throw—and, of course, he had that terrific arm that made him maybe the greatest threat ever to throw the ball down the field once he was on the move.

To this day, when you combine all of those immense physical skills, I can't think of a more dynamic quarterback in National Football League history than John Elway. Terry Bradshaw is a close second. In fact, if Terry were to come out in the NFL draft right now at the same age he was when the Steelers made him the top overall pick from Louisiana Tech in 1970, he would still be a physical marvel because of his size and the way he could throw the football. But I would still give the nod to Elway.

Steve McNair moves to throw down the field more than he did earlier in his career with the Oilers. So does Minnesota's Daunte Culpepper. His movement is becoming even more disastrous to defenses because he's moving to throw it deep down the field. Of course it helps when you have Randy Moss running those deep routes. And when it's third-and-6 and everyone is covered, Daunte still has the ability to run for a first down that breaks your back. And, oh, by the way, have you noticed that Donovan McNabb's running was down dramatically in 2003 and 2002 compared to what it was in 2001 and 2000? With each season he develops a better understanding that moving to gain more time to throw is usually more effective than moving to gain yards.

Peyton Manning is, by far, the most underrated mover among the league's current top quarterbacks. His footwork is so good, it borders on being great as far as maneuvering just enough to avoid the rush and being a more productive quarterback for Indianapolis. He is at the high end of that perfect blend that every team seeks. People give you credit as a running quarterback only when you make those highlight plays with your feet. Not enough credit is given to the quarterbacks who move around the pocket and shuffle to get extra time to throw. Right now, Peyton Manning is the master of that.

You can make a pretty good argument for New England's Tom Brady to rank fairly high up in that category as well. To say Brady is fast afoot would be one of the biggest lies in all of sports. Once during the 2003 season I talked with him about running out of the pocket, and he laughed and said, "Is there any quarterback in the NFL that's slower than me?" Tom wasn't giving himself quite enough credit. He is athletic enough, he is coordinated enough, and maybe most important of all, he is taught well enough by the Patriot coaches to move with the effectiveness he needs to buy that extra time.

Sure, a lot of that ability comes from instincts and feel, but it is taught. It's not just something you're born with. When I worked with Jim Fassel later in my career, he taught me about moving in the pocket. It was a revelation, because before, if I had to move, I would just turn and run and be out of position to throw the football. When you shuffle and you move, you must stay in the exact position that you would be in if you didn't have any pressure: shoulders parallel to the sideline, head turned down the field, toes facing the sideline in the perfect position to throw. Peyton Manning and Tom Brady do that exceptionally well.

How many more big plays are created with the quarterback moving in the pocket, giving himself that extra half second to throw, instead of running? If I had to put a number on it, I would say it is easily 10 to 1—and I'm being conservative.

"This quarterback might not have the physical abilities to successfully make the jump from college to the NFL, but you have to draft him because he has all the intangibles. . . . He's just a winner."

Nothing makes me want to lose my lunch more than this one. If you want to go by that logic, then John Elway was a horrendous college quarterback. He didn't have a winning record his last year at Stanford. He was in an offense that threw the ball, an offense that was built around him, and they lost. He was the top overall pick of the draft and will arguably go down as one of the best quarterbacks in the history of the National Football League, but all he did in college was lose.

Watching practice one day before a broadcast, I had a discussion on the sidelines with a team's personnel guy—who shall remain nameless—and he was telling me about all of these "intangibles" he was looking for in quarterbacks coming out of college. He couldn't quite specify what they were, but he said he would know them when he saw them.

After a while I said, "You know, you're going to look for that guy maybe for the rest of your life and you will never find him. But if you go out and find somebody that physically has qualities that give you a chance, you create a much greater margin for error and you will also find some of those other qualities you're talking about."

The physical qualities I was talking about are good size, a good throwing arm, and the ability to move reasonably well. Put those together with good, common intelligence and that gives you a lot of cushion where, if things don't go right, it can still work.

But if you find someone who is undersized and doesn't have a really good throwing arm, yet he has all of those intangibles that you're looking for—even though you can't always identify what they are—your margin for error is extremely small. You can put your finger on the physical qualities of players. When you start talking about how they handle pressure and other mental aspects, you're going into areas where there's no definitive answer.

I don't want to come across in this book as if I have all of the answers or that I come out on top in every football argument or discussion. Every weekend during the season, I can always count on a coach saying something to me that makes me say, "What was I thinking?" But as my conversation with this personnel person went on, he finally said, "You're right. That makes a lot of sense."

Unfortunately, sometimes quarterbacks who are physically gifted, who have all of the qualities you're looking for, don't realize the success in the NFL that you expect of them because they don't get with the right organization, coach, or surrounding cast. Take Jake Plummer as an example. He leaves Arizona, goes to Mike Shanahan in Denver, and now he's throwing more touchdowns than interceptions. Did Jake all of a sudden get really smart? Of course not. He probably doesn't even have the physical ability now that he had three years ago in Arizona. But when you combine his talent with better coaching, a better supporting cast and the offensive system that the Broncos run, you create an atmosphere for improvement.

Before a broadcast we did during the 2003 season, Jake mentioned that when he was with the Cardinals he couldn't understand, while watching TV highlights each Sunday, how quarterbacks from other teams were putting up numbers that he could only dream of. The answer was obvious: because he had to work so hard for them in Arizona. But in '03, Jake was the one putting up numbers at times that other quarterbacks could only dream of.

I'm not completely knocking the Cardinals here, but I would say the conditions surrounding him did have a lot to do with his struggles. He comes to the Broncos, who are organized and have a good franchise. The coach is creative. The Broncos can run the football. All of a sudden, he's faking handoffs to Clinton Portis (before he was traded to the Redskins), turning and throwing to Shannon Sharpe (before he retired to join our CBS team) or any other receiver who is 5 yards away, and that guy runs all the way to the end zone. And then Jake realizes that that's how you get a lot of touchdown passes.

What do you think Joe Montana and Steve Young used to say when they watched film of other quarterbacks going against a defense they were preparing to face? They probably said, "Look at what they're doing. That quarterback has no chance."

They must have had some good laughs. We'd play a team and go 10 for 20 throwing the ball. Joe Montana or Steve Young would play the same team the following week and go 27 of 32, and you'd ask yourself, *Is he really that much better than me?* (For my own ego, we won't answer that question.) It just comes down to talent, different circumstances, and different offensive approaches.

That is the reality of playing pro quarterback.

"You shouldn't play a quarterback as a rookie because it might ruin his confidence."

Name me the quarterback whose confidence was ruined because he played as a rookie, and I'll show you a quarterback who had no business playing at all. I just don't know that guy.

It is a game of adversity. It is a game of failure. I just don't think it's accurate to assume that throwing two interceptions in one game is going to destroy a rookie quarterback for the rest of his life. The things people say about what an athlete may be thinking are incredible.

You're made up of stronger stuff than that. When you drop back to throw you're thinking about forty things and throwing the ball. I never got ready to throw the ball and thought, *Ooo! This is a big throw. I've got to make it or my career will be ruined.*

Man, you just have to let the ball fly. It's not pro golf, where you stand over the putt and have a chance to think, *Well, if I make it, we win the Ryder Cup. If I miss it, I'm the goat.* That doesn't happen in football.

Yes, there are certain tensions that come with playing. But when it comes time for the talented young quarterback to play, it happens. All of that perceived thinking about how the guy's going to come apart when things get a little rough out there is fantasy. Even if you're a veteran superstar, you're going to encounter some turbulent times, but you live through it.

Coaches want their quarterbacks—and all their players, for that matter—to play with a sense of abandon, but while trying to keep their mistakes to a minimum. They want players on that tightrope, but they don't want them to fall. It's called playing on the edge, and it's the greatest attribute an athlete can have.

I actually learned about that concept one night as I sat in the stands at a high school basketball game next to an ex–pro basketball player. He was telling me about the fact he had been giving some instruction to a few of the kids we were watching. At one point he said to me, "If I'm the coach and I look at the stat line when the game is over, and my point guard has six assists and no turnovers, I'm not going to be happy. And I'm going to talk to him after the game."

I gave him an inquisitive look.

"Because if he has no turnovers," the former pro basketball player went on to say, "that means he wasn't playing fast enough, he wasn't just to the point of almost being out of control. That's when he's at his best.

"You've got to know when you're about to go out of control and pull it back just a little. I want my point guard to have twelve assists, but I also want him to have two or three turnovers, because if he's playing fast enough he's gonna make mistakes. You have to learn from them and pull back the next time."

As a quarterback you can't always play it supersafe or you'll never make the big plays. You have to take chances every once in a while. You have to find where that boundary is and how daring you can be.

We all get tougher from adversity. If I'm a coach or a general manager of a team and I draft a quarterback high, I'm going to get him on the field as fast as possible because I want to speed up the process of his learning and maturing so that he's ready to lead my football team sooner rather than later. Maybe you don't start the guy in week one of the NFL season because, realistically, you might need more preparation time so that he has a better chance for success. But by week five he should be at a stage where now he at least will not be a total detriment to your team.

Now, when you do make the decision to start a rookie quarterback, it does say that you're probably not a Super Bowl contender. There is no way that you can play the quarterback position and be at your best in your first year of the NFL because you just don't have the knowledge to take advantage of your physical skill.

Playing a rookie quarterback is important to his development and to the future of the team. It just comes down to how fast you want to push it along. There is no definitive answer to the question of when a rookie quarterback is ready to play. When the Giants traded for Eli Manning after the San Diego Chargers made him the top overall pick of the 2004 draft, they clearly chose him to eventually become their franchise player but they kept their options open by also signing a veteran in two-time NFL MVP Kurt Warner. You get a veteran quarterback because you still want to win games when you're trying to make that transition. Kurt Warner can slow that process down by playing extremely well.

Is it possible that someone of Eli Manning's stature could

sit on the bench the whole year? Yes. If Kurt Warner plays well enough and the Giants have enough success, then they will leave well enough alone. The perfect example is the Cincinnati Bengals, who in 2003 made Carson Palmer the top overall pick of the draft, and then went with Jon Kitna as their starter for the whole season. Kitna was playing well and the Bengals were in the play-off hunt, so they could not make the change. It wasn't that the Bengals were afraid of ruining Carson Palmer's confidence. They just did what gave them the best chance to succeed in that transitional period.

And that transition only lasted one year. Going into the 2004 season, Bengals coach Marvin Lewis named Palmer his starter.

"Quarterbacks get too much credit and too much blame."

Years ago that might have been true, but I don't believe that anymore—particularly in a society as impatient as the one in which we live. Quarterbacks in the league are taking much more blame than ever. I don't think it's even close.

With pro football being as high profile as it is and generating so much conversation on so many different fronts—Internet chat rooms, talk radio, newspapers, fantasy football—seemingly everyone has an opinion. Even extremely casual fans have something to say about a controversial decision or call somewhere during a game.

Sports talk radio started becoming big in the late '80s, and that changed things a little, but that was when you would find only one station like that in each town. Now in almost every market in the country there are multiple sports talk radio stations. What else are they going to talk about except the local teams? In NFL markets, the two biggest targets for second-guessing are the decisions of the quarterback and of the coach—in that order.

No one is under more scrutiny than the quarterback. The position is so visual; everyone can see everything the quarterback does. There are statistics that can be easily cited to back up every argument about his performance, good and bad. The point total, whether you won or lost . . . it all falls on the quarterback's shoulder pads.

The outside forces are absolutely much greater now than ever before. So are the inside forces. When teams lose, the other players are always willing to say—behind the quarterback's back, of course—that he's the reason they're losing. *It's not me; it's him.* Coaches are just as inclined to say the same thing. They're not as patient with quarterbacks as they used to be because they know, with the challenges of managing the salary cap and free agency causing constant roster turnover, there's no such thing as a five-year plan with a football organization anymore. Everything is a two-year plan, so you must win now.

"The quarterback is staring at the receiver too long."

If I hear this phrase a hundred times, it's probably true once. All right, maybe I'm underselling it a bit. Maybe it's true ten out of every hundred times.

Too often it's a crutch when trying to explain why a quarterback has a pass knocked down or he's throwing some incompletions. When you can't come up with a specific reason, you just say, "He's staring at the receivers way too long."

Let's think about the game from the quarterback's standpoint. Fifty percent of the time he's throwing against man-to-man coverage, which is when defenders are chasing the receivers. When they are chasing receivers they are not watching the quarterback, so they really do not know where he is looking.

When a quarterback can be guilty of staring at a receiver too long is against zone coverage, in which defenders are taught to drop back into an area of the field they're responsible to cover. They look at the quarterback and then also have to see what receiver comes into their area and will usually try to be alert to defend the pass if it comes toward him. But if, as the quarterback drops back, he looks to one side or the other, a defender's natural reaction, based on how he has been taught, is to take a couple of steps into the direction that the quarterback is looking. This is usually what is going on when a ball is thrown in the middle of the field and the linebacker is just in the right position to reach up with his hand and knock it down.

Another example of when a quarterback may be guilty of staring in one place too long would be when a safety is in the middle of the field. Often a safety has no one to cover; he is just responsible for an area of the field. But when a quarterback looks, the safety has the capability of reading the quarterback's eyes and running up to make interceptions wherever the quarterback happens to be looking.

Coaches constantly remind quarterbacks not to do this, of course. That's why, most of the time in the NFL, you will see a quarterback look one way and throw another pretty much in rhythm without wasting much time. When a quarterback is under the center, he can tell that the defense he's facing is going to play zone. And by looking one way and throwing another, he knows he can make that zone move two steps to the right or two steps to the left. As soon as that happens, the quarterback turns and throws to the opposite side. Now, instead of having three feet to throw the football into, he has six feet. That is called moving a defense with your eyes, but that only happens against zone coverage, and it doesn't happen that often.

One little trick that quarterbacks are always taught is to look right at that safety who is trying to read their eyes from the middle of the field. Once that happens, the safety can't do anything but stand right where he is. That's called freezing a defender. You freeze him, just for a split second. Now you've gained additional time to throw the ball in front of him or over his head or do whatever you're trying to accomplish on that play.

In the ten years I've been a broadcaster I have uttered the phrase, "The quarterback stared at his receiver too long," no more than five times. It just doesn't happen very often, especially in the NFL.

"The quarterback threw into double coverage."

I realize, up to this point, I've talked a lot about the quarterback, and maybe it seems as if I'm making excuses for the quarterback. I am not. But let's face it. I played the position for twenty-eight years, going all the way back to my grammar school days. We all think we know something, if not everything, about the quarterback. He does have the ball in his hands on every single play of the game, so a lot of attention has to go there, and we have no choice but to talk about him a great deal.

Some of that conversation comes in the form of praise; some comes in the form of criticism. And there are certain forms of criticism, such as "the quarterback threw into double coverage," that are way overused and often erroneous. Double coverage doesn't happen in pro football even close to the frequency that many people believe, especially nowadays, because there are so many different offensive formations that you simply can't defend with double coverage.

Look at the way the Minnesota Vikings use Randy Moss, probably the most talented wide receiver in the league. Most teams that face the Vikings would like to double-cover Randy Moss. Makes perfect sense, right? But what are you going to do if he lines up 2 yards outside of the tight end instead of out near the sideline, as he usually does? Do two defenders come running in there with him? What if he goes in motion to the other side? Do both of the defenders run with him?

What if he goes in motion, stops, and comes back? What if two other receivers line up right next to him? Who is going to cover whom when they all take off together? In most cases the Vikings are going to use formations to put Randy Moss in situations where it would be impossible or at least impractical for the defense to cover him with two people.

When you hear an announcer talk about a quarterback throwing into "double coverage," what you typically see on your TV screen is the free defender, usually the safety—who has no one to cover—reacting as he sees the quarterback put the ball in the air. As a gifted athlete he has the ability to run and get somewhat close to the ball as it reaches wherever the quarterback has thrown it. When it goes incomplete or is intercepted, the quarterback is criticized for his decision to throw into "double coverage."

If the ball gets batted into the air, that gives more defenders more time to get around the ball, like a bunch of piranhas converging on a chunk of raw meat. Then the announcer says, "Oh, my gosh! He didn't throw into double coverage. He threw into triple coverage." Never in my life have I seen triple coverage in pro football other than when a bunch of defenders are packed in the end zone to prevent a "Hail Mary" pass from being completed.

I will say that NFL announcers do face greater challenges in explaining all that's going on in a game because everything offensively and defensively has gotten more specialized and more unique. Even when I watch tapes of games, I have a hard time understanding who's covering whom and what's going on. But the good news is that I've heard "the quarterback is throwing into double coverage" less and less the last few years.

"The safety didn't get there in time."

This is the exact opposite of hearing that "the quarterback threw into double coverage." You generally hear this when a safety runs over to a side of the field and is just a step or two too late in making a play. The presumption is that he should have been part of the coverage, even though that usually is not the case.

As I mentioned earlier, a lot of times the safety in the middle of the field has more freedom to move wherever he is needed, so when the ball is thrown he reacts to it. If the ball is thrown long down the sideline, he runs in that direction, trying to get involved, even though it's not his responsibility. The receiver beats the defender who is supposed to be covering him, and the safety often ends up coming into the picture late to make the tackle. What's the next thing you hear out of an announcer's mouth? "The safety didn't get over there in time. The corner was expecting help."

But the safety is not making a mistake. He's making a tremendous play to save the corner's butt by helping to prevent a touchdown. He's not late at all. In fact, he did a hell of a job to get there. However, the announcers made the wrong assumption that the safety was part of the play. Because TV shoots it so tight, you can't always get the true picture. Unless the analyst who can see the play from a wide view tells us otherwise, we automatically conclude that the safety's having a bad game.

CHAPTER THREE

Looking for Those Dirty Little Secrets Is a Search Without End

didn't become serious about studying film until I got into the National Football League. If you were to add up all the time that I watched film of my opponents in high school, it wouldn't equal one hour. It just wasn't done at that level back in the early '70s. We barely even watched the films of our own games, let alone those of other schools. I probably saw all of five of my own high school games on film. When we did watch them I wasn't really doing it to learn anything. I was too busy watching myself and saying, "Wow! That's me up on the screen. Cool!"

I wasn't all that serious about film watching once I got to

.ollege, either, because there were so many variables involved, beginning with the fact that I was going to classes and I simply couldn't afford to be in a film room all the time. Besides, when I was playing quarterback for Morehead State, in Kentucky, I never got to a point where I felt that watching film was going to give me an advantage to win the game on Saturday. The game wasn't so complicated then that you needed to study it in any great detail. I don't remember worrying about a lot of coverages, blitzes, or any special players on the defense we were playing. It was, "Here's the play. Throw it to him."

We spent the majority of our time practicing, training on our own, and meeting, although most of the meetings were spent learning plays. In a normal week in college I probably watched an hour of film. And that's on the high end. Instead of staring at a screen we learned football situations on the field because we got such tremendous repetition of plays in practice. Of course, this was before the NCAA set time limits on how long you could practice and spend together as a football team during a week. We practiced for three hours, and I ran the offense almost the whole time. In the pros you get about 30 to 40 snaps a day for your offense. In college we were getting at least 100 a day.

About the only benefit I could ever get from watching film in college was an idea of the talent level of the team we were about to face. Almost all of my observations were about the physical prowess of players rather than strategic. There were not many deep thoughts.

I started to get a little more serious about it in 1979, my rookie year with the Giants, but it wasn't until 1984—the sixth year of my pro career—that I finally discovered all the benefits that watching film had for my career. After missing the 1982 season with a knee injury and losing my starting job to Scott Brunner in 1983, my career was in jeopardy. After he went 3-12-1 in his first season, Bill Parcells's career was in jeopardy, too. I'm sure that had a lot to do with his and his assistant coaches' stressing the importance of looking for even the tiniest edge we could find over our opponents. Bill would always tell us, "You've got to get here earlier. . . . You're going to have to watch more film. . . . You're going to have to pay a little more attention to detail. . . . You've got to study longer." In the eyes of the coaches, there really was no such thing as overworking.

It was about that time when Ron Erhardt, our offensive co-ordinator, started telling the quarterbacks to come to the stadium a little bit earlier than everybody else during the week. I'll never forget one day when we were getting ready to play the Washington Redskins, who had a good defense with guys like Dexter Manley and Charles Mann up front. I got to the stadium at about eight o'clock in the morning (players actually come in a lot earlier than that now, but it was early for that era), and as soon as I arrived, Ron told me to come to the meeting room because he had something to show me about the Redskins' defense.

"You're going to love this," Ron said, sounding proud of himself and almost giddy about what he was about to tell me.

"Okay, okay," I said. I tried to sound enthusiastic, but I was skeptical. In my mind I was saying, *Yeah, right, Ron. What is it you're going to show me that we haven't already seen? Another coverage?* I just couldn't imagine it would be that big of a deal.

I walked in the room, Ron threw on a film, and he pointed to the outside linebacker.

"Look at this," he said. "When his feet are parallel and he's somewhat head-up on the tight end, that tells you they're going to rush their four down linemen and play zone coverage. When he has one foot forward and the other foot back, it means it's a blitz."

"Oh, come on," I said. "That can't be true."

"Look."

Sure enough, when the outside linebacker had his feet parallel, he hit the tight end and then dropped back into zone coverage while only the four linemen rushed. Then, as Ron pointed out, I noticed that when the outside linebacker had his right foot forward and his left foot a good two or three feet behind him in a sprinter's stance, that meant a blitz was coming and there would be man-to-man coverage behind him.

"But that can't be true all the time," I said, still uncertain about just how great a revelation this was.

Ron looked at me and said, "It's a hundred percent."

"Man, that is cool," I said.

In the grand scheme of things it might not have meant anything to the outcome of the game. But in my mind, it meant something. It put me at ease because I could walk up to the line of scrimmage, take a quick look at that linebacker and think, *Here comes a blitz,* or, *It's zone coverage.* If it was man-to-man, I could make the read much faster and get rid of the football quicker.

All of a sudden it made me finally realize that I could gain some distinct advantages if I became a much better student of the game. I had watched a lot of film before then, but I don't think it ever really became a part of me until that year. I grew up, things became more definitive with the Giants, and all of a sudden it just wasn't about how hard and how far you could throw the ball. It wasn't all physical. You realize there's a mental side of the game and you want to take advantage of it.

It directly impacted the outcome of games. One reason was because I could recognize that a blitz was coming and do something about it. Another reason was that, because opposing defensive coaches and players knew I could recognize it and do something about it, they would dramatically change their strategy. We could play a team that blitzed a tremendous amount the week before, but they would play us and we wouldn't see any blitzing. The flip side of that is if you show a lack of blitz recognition, teams that never blitz will see that weakness and come after you. Everybody wants to join the party. Either way, having that ability to anticipate the blitz allowed me to make plays I ordinarily wouldn't have. And if I couldn't do that, we would have been in trouble.

The deeper understanding of the game that I started to develop went hand in hand with the fact our offense got a little more complicated. It got more sophisticated. We added more schemes. We went to more formations with three wide receivers, one tight end, and one back. We went to shotgun. We went with shotgun all the time on third down, which meant three wide receivers, one tight end, and one running back.

Those were things we kind of just dabbled in before, but now there were more passing plays. I was calling out protections at the line of scrimmage much more than I ever had before. The signals were simple. If we wanted the linemen to block to the left, I yelled, "Louie" or "Lucky." If we wanted them to block to the right, I said "Roger" and "Ringo." When you told the line to go right, the backs had to go left, opposite the line calls. That way, if a blitz was coming from the side opposite to where the line was moving, the running back could pick up the blitzer.

The system allowed me to have options. For instance, if I saw that two blitzers were going to come from my left side and the cornerback covering the wide receiver on that side was 8 or 9 yards off the line of scrimmage, I would not yell out "Louie" or "Lucky," which would have sent the linemen left along with somebody else to pick up the blitzers. Instead, I would let the line go right, and if it was third-and-6 or less, I could catch the shotgun snap, the wide receiver would see that two blitzers were coming from his side and would know—because we weren't going to pick up the blitzers—to change his route from a post pattern to a 6- or 7-yard out cut, and I could throw the ball to that receiver before the blitzers could knock me down or knock the football down, and still get the first down. It really was like stealing.

But there was one circumstance where I would make the call to pick up the blitz. If it was third-and-7 and that cornerback on the left side was up at the line of scrimmage—ready to bump the wide receiver—I would yell "Louie" or "Lucky" to send the line left and block the blitzers, then run the called play, a deep pass to one of the two receivers on the right side, and see if we could beat one-on-one coverage.

All of a sudden I realized there was another game inside the game, and that game was a lot of fun. When Ron would tell the quarterbacks, "Hey, look at what I found out," we were like kids. *Wow! This is great, Coach! You're awesome!* Ron would love it, too, because it would create energy among all of us. There was nothing like uncovering a dirty little secret about the defense.

Today I get to live those moments vicariously. During a production meeting before one of our broadcasts in the 2003 season, a defensive lineman confided in me about "some of the most unbelievable keys" he had found in the opposition.

"Really?" I said. "Well, tell them to me."

Without any hesitation he said, "For one, the heel of the quarterback's left foot comes up just a little tiny beat just before they snap the ball. So I'm just going to watch his left foot."

The other one he mentioned was one you hear a lot: If you see that an offensive lineman's back is flat, it's a run. If it's just barely tilted, with his shoulders just a little bit higher than his butt, it's a pass because he's getting ready to rock backward in pass protection.

We watched the game. The keys were 100 percent correct. He had them nailed. I didn't talk about them on the air because that's giving away information that that player could use when those teams play each other again. For that same reason I am not going to reveal the player's identity, the team he played for, or the game I broadcast.

All quarterbacks know that defensive players are constantly watching for and listening to everything they do, seeking that little change in their stance or voice inflection that will give something away. When defensive linemen—especially those lined up outside—get their heads low enough, they can see under the center's butt and watch the quarterback's hands. A lot of times the quarterback will flex his hands just before the snap, making them ridged because he's ready for the ball to hit them. You're talking about tenths of seconds, but you're looking for any edge you can get on the enemy.

Many quarterbacks have gotten to where they'll be under center and they'll flex their hands while they're calling signals to try to get those defenders who are trying to get that sneak peek to jump offside. But more important, that quarterback is trying to make sure the defense can't get a jump on the play that's going to be run.

It's like a silent snap count. You will almost always see it used when the quarterback is in shotgun formation and the crowd noise is too loud for the rest of the offense to hear his signals. You will see the center look through his legs at the quarterback, who will then raise one leg, and the center will yell out, "Set!" as loud as he can so that the other offensive linemen can hear it. Once the center yells "Set!" everyone counts in his head, "One thousand and one," and then the ball will be snapped.

NFL teams do this so often that defensive linemen have gotten used to it and have come up with an antidote. When they hear the center yell, "Set!" they count "One thousand and one" to themselves, and go. Now, of course, offenses realize that defenses are doing this, so in response they use silent snap counts on one, two, and three. For instance, a silent snap count on two means that the center looks through his legs, the quarterback raises one leg, the center lifts his head and yells "Set!"

but it doesn't mean anything. He pauses, looks through his legs again and for the second time, the quarterback raises his leg. The center again lifts his head and yells, "Set!" and this time the linemen count to themselves, "One thousand and one" and the ball is snapped.

Ron Erhardt did a good job of keeping me aware of my own tendencies to help prevent me from unknowingly giving any tips to opposing defenses. One day he came down to the locker room and told me that on every pass play my feet were not parallel before the snap. At first I didn't think it was true because when I played I didn't believe in having a funny stance. I'd always set my feet the same way, keeping them parallel, but when we watched the film, there was the proof.

At the time my right ankle was extremely sore, so to compensate for my limitation of movement I was sneaking my right foot back to try to get away from the center a little bit quicker. Suffice it to say that I got out of that habit quickly, because I was sure the defensive linemen we would face that week were going to pick up on my unusual stance and become a little quicker in their pass rush. They knew it wasn't going to be a straight running play or a draw. They knew it was going to be a pass, and I would pay the price.

So much of this game is simply about mannerisms and body language, just a lot of basic human behavior that can reveal more about a player's intentions than he would want his opponent to know. Sometimes it was just a look that defensive players had that let me know a blitz was coming. You could feel the sense of urgency in their actions. Other times I would get up underneath the center and there would be two linebackers, one on each side of the center. They'd be gesturing and grunting as if they were going to rush, but I knew they weren't blitzing because they were overacting. Basically, they just weren't good enough actors. They didn't convince me, and most of the time I was right not to buy into their pathetic performance.

So many times players don't think you notice little things they're doing. An example: Don't you like going to a party and someone comes up to you trying to act like they haven't been drinking, but you can take one look at them and say, "My gosh! You've already had four or five beers." Sometimes on a football field it's no different. It reminds me of a story from 1982. I was hurt and was upstairs in a booth watching the Monday-night game between the Giants and Packers. Lynn Dickey was the quarterback for Green Bay at the time. Mike Mayock was a rookie strong safety for us. He was at the line of scrimmage, waving his arms around. Then he pointed to the cornerback, as if to say, "You and me are going to double this receiver who is close by us."

As Mike did all this he tried not to look at Dickey, because what Mike was really doing was faking the double coverage and he was going to blitz. Mike didn't want Dickey to see or think he was coming on the blitz. Right before the snap, Mike couldn't stand it any longer. He had to look at the quarterback, just out of the corner of his eye. Sure enough, Dickey was looking right at him. Then he gave Mike a little wink, as if to say, "Yeah, I know you're blitzing. You're doing all of that arm waving, trying to disguise it, but it's not working. I know you're coming with the blitz."

At the time Dickey was a ten-year veteran and had seen it all, so there was no way a rookie strong safety was going to fool him with some bad first-year antics straight from a second-rate movie. As Mike later told me, it was a humbling, terrible feeling to know it was that easy for a quarterback to see through all his actions.

A question I'm asked all the time is, "When did it all come together for you mentally as a quarterback?"

I don't know exactly what year it was, but there came a point where I could look across the line and see the smallest details that told me the defense was about to do something different than usual. That was crucial, because it took away the doubt in my mind and the element of surprise from the defense. When that happens for a quarterback, he's able to make quicker and smarter decisions because he's figured out something the defense has plotted to catch him off guard.

A good example would be this: The Dallas Cowboys' safeties usually were 9 to 9.5 yards off the line of scrimmage. Now, when I got underneath the center and saw that those safeties were 8 to 8.5 yards from the line, I knew a blitz was coming. I'm sure you're thinking, *Come on, Phil, are you telling me you can see a subtle difference like that on a football field?*

Absolutely. After so many years of watching film, playing experience, teaching from coaches, repetitions in practice, that 1 yard to me would be like 10 yards to the average person. That's how obvious looking at safeties in that situation was.

I wasn't big on taking film home because what environment is better for study and concentration than the one created for us at the team's complex? There at my fingertips I had big video screens and every imaginable tape of the opponents. I didn't have any kids running around making noise or the phone ringing to interrupt me. It's also pretty quiet at the stadium, because most of the other players would leave between 4 and 4:30 P.M. after practice.

When I came home, around 6:30 or 7 o'clock at night, I wanted to be free. I wanted to lay around with my kids. I wanted to eat some of my wife's great cooking. I didn't even study my playbook much at home at night. Besides, if you live in—or have spent any time driving through—the state of New Jersey, you'll understand that I actually could do a lot of studying in my car. On a good day the sixteen-mile commute between Giants Stadium and my home in Franklin Lakes took thirty-five minutes, but usually it was an hour. As my car crawled along Route 3, then up Route 17 and onto Route 208, I'd have my playbook open on the passenger seat and I'd memorize plays and formations.

To give you an idea of just how challenging an assignment that could be, we could have as many as a half dozen formations just for one off-tackle run. With 10 to 12 runs per game, and anywhere from 50 to 60 passes per game, you're talking about a lot of memorization for the quarterback. The formations and movements in our offense were just endless, and we had to have all of them committed to memory, because back then there was no electronic communication system by which the coach could talk into a microphone and the quarterback would hear him inside his helmet. A coach had to flash in the formations and plays with hand signals from the sideline. For us that person was Ray Handley, our running backs coach at the time. There wasn't time for him to give eighteen hand signals, so he came up with an abbreviated language that all the quarterbacks had to know because, through injury or poor performance, any one of us could be under center at any given time.

Saturday morning was quiz time for the quarterbacks to make sure we knew all the formations, plays, and corresponding hand signals. Ray Handley loved quizzing us, and he took great joy in making every single play as difficult as he possibly could. A typical question would go like this: "Okay, Phil, if you have two tight ends, two running backs, one wide receiver and we run off tackle, what's the formation?" Keep in mind, that same play could be run with three wide receivers, one back, and one tight end. Or one tight end, two backs, and two wide receivers. Or three tight ends, one back, and one wide receiver. In addition, some of those personnel groupings would have multiple formations for that off-tackle run, and some of them only had one formation. The mind-bending task was trying to figure out what that one formation was.

Ray had all of our names written on a big grease board behind him, and whenever you got an answer wrong he would pull out his blue marker and put a big slash under your name. It would always be a contest between the quarterbacks to see who could get the fewest wrong. And we would be like fifth-graders in rejoicing when one of us didn't know an answer. Two of the quarterbacks would actually give each other high-fives when the other guy got one wrong. Can you imagine grown men, making all that money, acting like a bunch of schoolkids?

But that provided a little extra incentive to study hard and make sure you had all that information down cold.

CHAPTER FOUR

Countdown to Sunday: Six Days of Endless Chatter . . . Then You Get a Microphone

A **lot of my old friends** from college, especially ones that didn't know me well, look at me today and say, "We can't believe you actually go on TV and talk."

It befuddles them to no end because they knew me as a person who wasn't outgoing. They didn't know me as the person I became when I was on the field. I've heard it said many times that when you put on a disguise you can act the way you are supposed to. That's what a football uniform did for me. I acted the way I was supposed to in a football uniform—or in a baseball uniform, for that matter. When I was growing up, baseball was my first love. I was a pitcher, and played third, first, and shortstop. All the people I grew up with, people I was around, thought that baseball was my sport. And it was, until college, when I decided to devote more time to football.

I never said too much in classes or at parties. However, my teammates in college and the closer friends I had back then weren't surprised that I ended up in an announcer's booth, because they would hear my endless chatter on the field or in the locker room or wherever we would be hanging out and talking sports.

For me that's pretty much what the broadcast business is all about: endless chatter. And not just when I'm behind a microphone. The talking I do during those three hours each Sunday doesn't compare to the amount of talking I do all week in the course of preparing for a telecast.

The process begins on Monday morning when, just like a player, you rehash the game you've just done. I talk by phone with the producer, director, and my partner (who until 2004 was Greg Gumbel; he moved to host's chair on the *NFL Today* set, while Jim Nantz moved next to me in the booth). Basically, the questions we address with each other are: How do you think we did? Did we cover it well? Did we talk about the right subjects? What was the rating for the game? Although I don't believe we, as a broadcast crew, have anything to do with the ratings, you always want to know what they are because you always get excited about what it means to the network when you have big numbers.

Like a player you always hate yourself on Monday. You

always second-guess yourself, pointing out things you forgot to mention on the air even though that was your intention all week, or things you could have said so much better than you did. The second-guessing is almost even worse than what I did when I was playing, because as a player you could find a lot of good after a win. With a broadcast you don't have a definitive outcome. Our idea of doing it exceptionally well and being proud of what we did doesn't necessarily agree with what someone else might think of our performance. Even though we thought we had a good broadcast, there are media critics who sometimes think otherwise. It's all very subjective.

I spend the rest of Monday talking with people around the league and comparing notes of what went on in Sunday's games. I'll also hear from radio stations that want me to talk about the game I saw and things happening elsewhere in the NFL. I enjoy doing those interviews because it provides another forum to express my opinions and maybe get some different ideas.

One of my favorites is the weekly segment I do by phone during the season with Don Imus on WFAN in New York and broadcast nationally on the Westwood One Network. Don is an average sports fan who casually watches games on TV. He knows a little bit about everything, which is exactly what we talk about. Not necessarily the Giants. Not necessarily about the NFL at all. You never know where our conversation is going to go week to week. Don will usually say something derogatory about my announcing or make fun of my appearance on the screen in the previous week's game, noting how much weight I've gained and that sort of thing. It's fun.

Tuesday I receive videotape of the game we just did. Early in my broadcast career I used to watch the entire game to listen to everything I said, but not anymore. I usually fast-forward to two or three crucial moments of the game, where a lot was going on, and I ask myself, *Did I make sense of what was going on?* Much the way Ron Erhardt would do with me when I was playing, I look for flaws and tendencies that might be taking away from my performance, such as unconsciously overusing a particular word or phrase. Warner Wolf, a former sportscaster for WCBS-TV in New York, will call me periodically to let me know about any bad habits he detects from me in our broadcast. I remember once when he alerted me to my frequent use of, "I mean" to set up a particular point I was making. Sure enough, when I checked the tape of the broadcast I discovered that I was saying, "I mean" before just about every other thought.

When I was with NBC, Dick Ebersol, the president of NBC Sports, called our producer, Tommy Roy, on the "hot line" in our production truck during one game to mention that whenever I singled out a key portion of a replay I was in the habit of saying, "Right there!" Once someone points out something like that, you're conscious of it and sometimes it's hard to speak naturally when you're trying not to say a certain word or phrase. The following week I was convinced I had it under control, but just before halftime Tommy pushed the button that allowed me to hear him in my earpiece.

"Phil, I just got a call from New York," he said. "Dick Ebersol said to tell you that you're setting records for how many times you're saying, 'Right there' this week."

●　　●　　●

Tapes of the previous games played by the teams we will be covering in our next telecast also arrive on Tuesday, and I spend a couple of days watching them. I want to see what the scene was like, what conditions the games were played under. You can see human things from TV tapes, such as facial expressions. I get a clean view of the football. Coaches' tape is shot from far away. You can see all the players at once, where everyone is positioned and where and how everyone moves. But you can't quite see the details that you can from a television tape, such as the flight of the football.

As Donovan McNabb and the Philadelphia Eagles were struggling early in the 2003 season he had a thumb that was bothering him a little. By watching the TV tape I could see, without question, the effect the injury was having on his ability to throw the ball. When a quarterback throws properly, the nose of the football is slightly up in the air. Think about it aerodynamically. When the nose is up a little, the ball glides through the air. If the nose is down a little, it only makes sense that the ball has a better chance of reaching the ground before it gets to the receiver's hands. That was what was happening on quite a few of McNabb's passes.

I want to understand how each game unfolds—how the tight game is won or lost—so that I can get a feel for what to expect when we see the same teams play. I want to hear what the announcers have to say about the players and coaches so we don't repeat the same stuff. As I watch, I make notes about any number of thoughts that hit my mind. They could be about play calling. They could be about the design of plays. They could be about techniques I notice that are giving certain players success, or maybe I'll pick up on a technique that a player is doing wrong.

I study the media packets I receive from both teams: rosters, press releases, newspaper clippings, and literally hundreds upon hundreds of stat sheets. I go on the Internet to read the local papers of the teams we're going to see, just to get an idea of what other people are saying about them.

Endless chatter. Sometimes you've got to be careful not to allow yourself to get too caught up in it, especially when it's mostly negative. Sometimes you've got to be careful, when you watch a game and Team A throws for 300 yards against Team B, not to assume automatically that Team B's defense is bad. The front seven could be winning the war, but you could have a breakdown with a defensive back that ends up allowing big yardage, so it creates a misconception.

In week two of the 2003 season we had New England at Philadelphia. In week one, Buffalo beat New England, 31–0. I'm like a fan. I've got some built-in preconceptions. Before I looked at stats or saw tapes of the game my first thought when I saw that lopsided score was, *Bill Belichick's been doing some unique stuff the last couple of years. I guess it's easier to catch on to now. Teams have figured it out and the Patriots are going to get ripped up. Maybe people have figured out New England's defense, and they're in for a long year.*

Complicating matters was the fact that five days before the game the Patriots released safety Lawyer Milloy, a very popular player with fans and teammates. Some Patriot players were very public in expressing their shock and disappointment over Milloy's departure—and the fact the Bills promptly picked him up and had him in uniform to face his former team. There were all kinds of media speculation, in New England and nationally, that the players were so upset with Belichick, they had actually staged a mutiny in that Buffalo game.

Then I watched the broadcast tape of that game. At halftime I had already come to the conclusion that the preconceptions I had—based on the score and all the discussion surrounding Milloy—were wrong. I was even more certain of that after I saw the whole game. Drew Bledsoe made a couple of throws that were backbreakers that only he could make—that most other quarterbacks in the league wouldn't even attempt. But he threw them because he had patience. He threw them because he was big enough to stand in the pocket and could shake off the pass rusher and then, on first-and-20 from his own 11, throw a ball 49 yards on a line to a receiver down the middle of the field. That helped set up his short touchdown pass to give the Bills a 14–0 lead. Buffalo put the game away when nose tackle Sam Adams suddenly turned into a 335-pound cornerback and rambled 37 yards with an interception return for a touchdown.

You know how finicky the whole NFL is, and you begin to remind yourself that the game was up in Buffalo. It was the season opener. There was a lot of added fuel, from a highly emotional crowd, for the home team. Let's be careful how we judge this. Let's not be so quick to send one team to the Super Bowl or write the other one off.

Even some of the Patriot defensive backs we spoke to about Bledsoe's performance said, "Man, that was just sick." They were so upset because they knew that maybe only Drew could have made that 49-yard throw, and that was frustrating to them. But they were all over the Bills at the line of scrimmage.

The game kind of got out of hand. The Bills got some breaks on third downs when there were some penalties that ended up leading to some of their scores.

The more I talked with some of the Patriot players, the more I could see that although the Lawyer Milloy thing bothered them, they still loved Bill Belichick. They believed in this guy. He led them to the Super Bowl. They still wanted to soak in everything he said every week. Why? Because what he tells them gives them a great chance to win.

I put it all together and realized that the Patriots had a good defense and the numbers weren't that out of whack in week one. They weren't 31-0 numbers, that was for sure. When I watched the tape, I judged the physical battles up front. I could see that the Patriots' defense was absolutely winning a lot of those battles.

On one of my national radio appearances, I told the host, "You're going to think I'm crazy, but listen to me here. I was really impressed with New England's defense in week one."

"Ah, come on, Phil," he said, obviously thinking that I was, in fact, off my rocker.

"I'm telling you, I saw a physically dominating defense."

I don't want to say I told you so—wait, yes I do. The Patriots, and especially their defense, dominated the Eagles, 31-10. I won't say I projected the Patriots to go on to win another Super Bowl because such a prediction that early in the season is as silly as saying their season was over after one game.

But I will pat myself on the back for not jumping to conclusions and for taking a look at another side of the story.

•　　•　　•

Friday morning always entails an extremely early flight to the city where we're broadcasting the game. We want to arrive at the home team's complex in time to watch coaches' film, watch practice, and talk to the head coach, a couple of assistant coaches, and generally four players—two from offense, two from defense—that we requested earlier in the week.

Friday practice is when teams rehearse a lot of the specific plays they're going to use in the game. You'll notice that there were a lot of passes to a particular player, and you say, *That's interesting. They think he's going to be open quite a bit.*

Later on we do the coach and player interviews at the home team's complex (we meet with the visiting team's coaches and players at their hotel, right after they arrive from the airport). There are no cameras or microphones in these sessions. These are just casual conversations around a table with our crew, between twenty minutes and an hour with the coach and about ten to fifteen minutes with each player.

We're looking for everything—personality, stories that we can share on Sunday that we can have a little fun with or be serious about, what's been right or wrong with the team, what's going to change, what they're hoping to do. You can't get enough.

Sometimes coaches will let us in on a trick play they're planning to use so that we can keep an eye out for it. I won't say anything specific on the air until after they do it, because someone from the other team might be listening when you say, "They're going to run a flea-flicker here." Of course, after the play is run, we'll usually mention that the coach gave us the heads-up on it.

After I watch tapes I don't have to ask the coach if his quarterback is making good decisions because I can watch the film and know. Sometimes coaches don't want to say bad things about some of the players. With a quarterback they're usually not going to say, "Yeah, he's making stupid decisions." Their livelihood is tied too closely to the guy and they don't want to throw it out there to the public that he's struggling.

But I know the progression that the quarterback's supposed to be following. All I have to see is what the play is designed to do, and I can tell you that he's supposed to look at the halfback, then the wide receiver, and that the tight end coming across is his third guy. I can figure that out as soon as I see the tape, and I know if he has made the right or wrong decision. I don't need anybody to tell me that.

I also don't need anyone to tell me about what sort of chemistry a team has. When you watch players on film and at practice and you gather other information—by talking to the coach, or by talking to the players about themselves, or to the players about one another—you can get a good read on them. You can get a sense of the coaches, too. You see what makes them different. You see how they interact with the players, how everything works together.

As a broadcast crew we walk away from many games or organizations saying, "They are so close to being a contender." Or, "It's just not working for these guys."

With certain organizations the energy is no good. You can just sense it from certain words players use when talking about other players—and, maybe just as important, what they don't say about the other players. You can sense a true, deep-down dislike for their coach, even if they won't say so, which almost always is the case. There are negative feelings you get from watching practice or watching film. You just see fundamental breakdowns that aren't there if you have your house in order. Those are all signs that a team is eventually going to crumble.

If I took my neighbor from up the street—someone not connected with football in any way—on no more than a half dozen of my trips for CBS each season, he could tell me the three teams that are going to be successful and the three that are not—even if he didn't know their records or the players or the teams. Sometimes it's that simple to see.

What makes a restaurant great? Is it just the food or does the atmosphere have something to do with it? You liked the perfect lighting. You liked the color scheme of the walls and the decorations and the furniture. You liked the way the hostess talked to you. You liked the way the waiter served the food to you. The food might not have been the best, but you perceived it to be better than it was because the atmosphere was so outstanding. That sort of thinking can hold true for a football team as well.

To take the analogy further, that same exact plate of food you ate could be served to you in ten different restaurants and it would taste different in each one. Now think of football. You could have ten teams run the exact same play, but the way it's presented to the players and the way the players perceive it are going to be different with each team. I've had the same plays delivered to me by different coaches. When certain coaches gave it to me, I'd believe in my heart that it was good stuff. With others I'd think, *Ah, this is just another bad play he's putting in.*

A coach once told me that he thought the importance of

team chemistry was overrated. He put it in the most fundamental way he could: "You've got good chemistry when you win and bad chemistry when you lose." I don't agree with that. I believe too strongly in human beings to ever think it could be as simple as that. I think the right mix of people working together creates winning, whereas the wrong mix of people just creates a bad atmosphere and it probably causes you to lose sometimes when you shouldn't.

Almost every single time we meet with a coach before a broadcast, the first thing he talks about is the chemistry of his team—how everyone works together, the "good guys" and "bad guys" that are on the roster. As Bill Parcells would always say, "You've got to get rid of the rats on your team." A rat is a player who is a divisive force in your locker room. He complains about everything, especially the coach. He thinks he knows more than everyone else. At the first sign of trouble he is the easiest guy to find, because rats always are the first to jump ship. When you're that kind of a person, you become a germ—and the germ always spreads.

When you have good chemistry you're surrounded by people with the same beliefs as yours. They want to do their job the correct way. They don't want to disappoint their teammates. They don't want to disappoint the coach. The rats are the guys who say, "Hey, I'll just do my job. I'll just take care of me. You worry about yourself."

You want your players to feel good about what you're doing. You want the energy. You want everybody to feed off one another. It's not just about working hard. It's more than that. It's working harder on the field than even the most dedicated person wants to work. It's studying more than even the most dedicated person wants to study. It's putting in more time than even the happiest guy to play football wants to put in. The only way to accomplish all of those agendas is to have people who can get along with each other and who don't say things or create an atmosphere that would divide the team.

Our 1986 Super Bowl team was a perfect example. We had great camaraderie and closeness. To this day, many of us remain friends. Winning always helps team chemistry, but even if that team hadn't been as successful as it was, we still would have gotten along well and would be friends.

Most coaches have been in the business long enough to know that they don't want or need problem children. It's too hard of a job, there's too much work to deal with the problems off the field or the problems certain players can create in the locker room. The ones who do pick up those kinds of players know they're gambling, it costs them, and they always regret doing it. When you compromise your principles it usually is a sign of desperation and it almost always shows up in the loss column. It's inherent in all coaches to think that they can always get the very best out of their players, but when they're wrong about a problem child it's a problem. A big problem.

Think of two classrooms. In one you have twenty students who listen to the teacher and interact with the teacher and have a little give-and-take with the teacher. In another class you also have twenty students, but two of them are throwing things, hitting other kids when the teacher's not looking, talking out loud and making other noise. Which class has a better chance to learn the most that day? It's the same with a football team.

Are there instances when taking a talented but high-risk player can work? Yes. I'll never forget how, in 1997, when Bill Parcells took over the New York Jets, it was widely assumed that one of his first moves would be to get rid of Keyshawn Johnson, who had just written an inflammatory book called *Just Give Me the Damn Ball!* Bill has written some books of his own, but it wasn't much of a stretch to assume he wouldn't appreciate Keyshawn's brand of literature, especially when it could easily be perceived as an order—not a request—to the coaching staff. The last time I checked, Bill was not in the habit of giving players much input on designing game plans or calling plays.

There was a part of me that was as skeptical as everyone else that it wouldn't work with Keyshawn Johnson, but I had the privilege of watching Bill Parcells work with Lawrence Taylor for eight years, and if you're a drinking man, you would know that Keyshawn Johnson is a Shirley Temple next to Lawrence's double dry martini. Without a doubt, Bill got more out of Taylor than any other coach in the National Football League could ever have dreamed of. There wasn't another Jets player more loyal to Bill Parcells than Keyshawn Johnson. In every TV close-up of Bill and Keyshawn on the sideline, you could always see Keyshawn within earshot, hanging on every single word and thought that came out of Bill's mouth.

When Keyshawn doesn't feel that kind of connection, he can be a divisive force on a football team, because he will make his displeasure known to anybody and everybody who will listen. After his act wore thin in Tampa Bay in 2003, it made perfect sense for him to reunite with Bill in Dallas for various reasons. One, Bill definitely understands him. Two, Keyshawn respects

Bill like no one else. Three, Bill the football coach still sees that there is something in Keyshawn's ability that is going to help make the Cowboys a better team.

Plus, who would be better at spreading the gospel according to Parcells throughout a locker room, to the media, to the fans than Keyshawn Johnson?

CHAPTER FIVE

Coaching:
A Wicked World That Some of Us
Can Resist and Some of Us Can't

"When you're a leader of men, that's what you do. I
believe that's what I am. That's what Bill Parcells is.
That's why you get back in."

—Dick Vermeil, Kansas City Chiefs coach

A **s thorough as I think** I might be in my mental preparation for a broadcast, I would say it is nowhere even
close to the preparation necessary for playing in a game. In pro
football terms it's laughable how little homework there is in
broadcast preparation. As a player I put in at least twice the
amount of preparation time that I would in a whole week for a
broadcast.

When you're preparing as a player you get extremely specific about situations, opposing players, and what you're trying to accomplish. You know the consequences are so much greater. It can be the difference between winning and losing. It's your job. It's your life.

When preparing for a broadcast, I look at film much more in generalities than I did as a player. I don't have to sit there and keep going back and forth on every single play until I wear out the buttons on my remote control. I'm just looking to get general thoughts to share with an audience that is a lot more casual in its knowledge of the game compared to anyone in a team environment.

Being a broadcaster is a wonderful occupation, but it doesn't require you to know every last detail, because at the end of the day you're not being judged on the basis of a victory or loss. You're not being second-guessed anywhere near as much as the players and coaches. In broadcasting you want to make sure you're understood by a broader range of people with varying degrees of understanding of the game.

As an announcer I don't even watch a game as I did when I was a quarterback. I react to what I see and sometimes antici- pate what I think I might see every once in a while. But when you're in the middle of the action, the game is too fast and there are too many variables to think you can watch it as a broadcaster or as a fan. Most of the time I'll make references to what I saw a team do in its previous game or in practice or to what the coaches tipped me off to regarding a particular situa- tion of the game.

Through the years I've started looking at broadcasts much

more from the fans' perspective. Viewers can't follow too much. They can understand when you're talking about positions such as quarterback, running back, the receivers, and so forth. But once it gets past the simplest of forms, you're wasting your breath and time.

I always try to remember that at some point I'm going to be talking to someone who knows very little about football, so I have to speak in a way that they, too, can understand what I say. I try to stay away from buzz terms such as "Two Deep" or "Eight in the Box." Instead of "Eight in the Box," I'll talk about the defense "crowding the line of scrimmage" to stop the run.

Who except those with a deep understanding about football would know what I was saying if I talked about a "Six Technique" or a "Nine Technique"? Those are natural football terms, and in the football world we all use them regularly. However, when your audience numbers in the millions and includes a very small percentage of coaches and players, you shouldn't just recite them as if everyone is going to know what you're talking about. Many times I think announcers do that just because they think it makes them sound knowledgeable.

A typical question fans have is, "Is the game as complicated as everyone says it is?" My standard answer is, "No, it's not. It's much, much more complicated than that."

Coaches and players work harder now than anyone could ever imagine. All the time the NFL workday seems to start earlier and earlier. Coaches are showing up at the office long before the sun comes up. Players arrive for meetings first thing in the morning. When my NFL career began in 1979, I think our first meeting as a team was at 10 A.M. Ray Perkins, our coach at the time, was a big meeting guy. The quarterbacks were in at 8:30 or 9 o'clock, and we would meet for an hour, sometimes an hour and a half, before the rest of the team got there.

The NFL changed a lot during the players' strike of 1987, because after we came back to work we had to do a lot of cramming to make up for all the lost time. Coach Parcells moved up our team meeting an hour, to 8:30. The quarterbacks' meeting was pushed an hour before that, and the next thing you knew, we were having meetings that started at 7:30 to 8 o'clock in the morning.

The strike also gave us walk-throughs, which are now standard with every team in the NFL. Our team meeting would basically be from 8:30 in the morning to 11. Just before we broke for lunch we would walk out on the field, just in our sweats, and we rehearsed plays and situations that we talked about in the meetings and saw on film all morning long. The idea was to squeeze additional on-field work into our compressed post-strike schedule. I would take the snap, drop back to the position I was supposed to finish in, and I would go through the motion of throwing the ball to the receiver down the field. Most of the time the ball would never actually leave my hand. It truly was a dry run of all the plays and situations we were going to execute fully that afternoon in practice. Those rehearsals were so beneficial to the players and coaches they just became a permanent part of NFL life.

I was further reminded of the crazy hours coaches keep when I was at the Denver Broncos' offices one Saturday morning before a 2003 broadcast. Gary Kubiak, the Broncos' offensive coordinator, told me, "I really like what you're doing on TV. I can tell you're working hard."

I appreciated the compliment, but I couldn't help but start laughing.

"Now, Gary," I said, "are we talking about working hard in my world or your world?" Gary laughed, too, because he knew, as I did, how absurd the comparison was.

That same day in the Broncos' offices I saw Steve Watson, the former Denver receiver who had been a successful businessman and was now coaching the Bronco receivers. It was around 8 o'clock in the morning, supposedly on a fairly easy workday for all NFL coaches. When I stuck my head in Steve's office I noticed he looked pretty busy.

"Steve, what time did you get in here this morning?" I said.

He looked up, gave me this sheepish grin, and said, "Five-thirty."

The life of a coach is unreal. I don't know if I can truly say that I could have been one if I wanted to because I don't even want to be that presumptuous. I always did think about coaching, but I don't know if I ever was serious about it. I don't know if I ever was fully committed to the idea of being a coach.

I get embarrassed when people say, "Wow! You follow the game so closely, you could be a coach." My face will actually turn red. I know they mean well, but I can't even respond to a comment like that. What I want to say to them is, "Any coach in the NFL would laugh in your face for saying that because they know, and I know, that that is so untrue."

In fact, what I always tell myself is, *Thank God, this broadcasting thing came along, because I might have been coaching.* Not that coaching wouldn't have been fulfilling. I might have loved it and I did see it as a possibility after I was done playing. The fact is, while I played I never thought much about what I would do when I retired. Coaching was always a possibility, but I think I was anxious to see if there was something else that might be out there for me.

I did know that coaching was a wicked world. I can't tell you how many times I've come home from broadcasting an unbelievable game that comes down to the last play, and hear my wife, Diana, say, "That was a great game today. But, oh, what about those poor players and coaches on the losing team? Football is such a heartbreaking business. If you're in it, there's no doubt you're going to get your heart broken."

I would agree with her, saying, "Thank God that we're out of that part of the business."

I'm also thankful that I had those fifteen years as a player and can live on the memories. It's just tough to see how games are lost sometimes. Yeah, I know I'm not going to get that high of winning a football game probably ever again and, believe me, that feeling is so great that you can't duplicate it. But I don't have to deal with all the heartache, either, that comes with losing a football game.

When I was playing and we lost I'd carry that loss at least until Wednesday, when we started practicing for the next game. I'd become sullen. I didn't talk very much. It was terrible, especially when you'd lose and you'd know that you were one of the big factors in losing. I would relive the game constantly—go over every bad throw, every bad decision that I made as a quarterback. You have a very hard time sleeping. The only way to wash away those memories was to start working on the next opponent, which usually began on Wednesday.

Living in the New York area, I regularly follow the Giants and the Jets. Think about the Giants in 2003, losing to the Eagles on a last-second punt return. How about the Giants' second game of that '03 season against Dallas on *Monday Night Football*? They're leading by 3 points with fourteen seconds left in regulation and they squib the kickoff out of bounds. That gives the Cowboys one last shot from their 40. They take advantage of it, tie the game up, go into overtime, and they win. If the Giants had only squibbed that kick inbounds the game would be over. How would you like to go home and try to sleep on that? I can't imagine.

With coaching you can't just stick your toe in and test the water. It's not the sort of business that allows you to breeze in and think you can just dabble in it a few hours a day. You've got to jump in the deep end right away. When players leave the field and go into coaching, they are in for such a shock, because it's not like anything they've ever experienced in their lives.

Maurice Carthon, a former fullback with the Giants and a good friend of mine whom I think is going to be a head coach in the NFL someday, once told me, "Man, that first year, it is so tough getting used to those long hours. Many times we'd be sitting around the conference table, in a coaches' staff meeting, and you'd fall right asleep. You're looking right at the coach, and the next thing you know, you're asleep because you just can't help it, you are so tired."

Mark Bavaro, our All-Pro tight end with the Giants, briefly tried his hand at coaching as a special assistant on Bill Parcells's Jets staff in 1997. He was brought in to help out with the tight ends just during training camp. Mark discovered right away that he did not like the hours, but even worse, was sitting through staff meetings and hearing the exceptionally harsh comments that the coaches made during their evaluations of players on the team. At the end of one of those meetings, he said, "My gosh! Did you coaches talk about us the same way when I was playing for the Giants?" They all laughed, and one of them said, "Oh, no, Mark, we only said good things about you guys." Sure they did.

That kind of culture shock doesn't just happen to an ex-player. It also happens to former college coaches when they get their first taste of NFL coaching as well.

For many years I kept all the playbooks and notepads from my playing career. If Ron Erhardt handed me ten passing plays to study, I would go over the details of everyone's assignment, including my own, on each play. But I'm a big believer in writing information down, because that helped me to learn, and that was where the notepads came in. I would draw up a play as it was illustrated in the playbook, write the formations below it, and then I would write all of my comments below that. I ended up with many notepads filled with detailed notes about why I liked a particular play, why we were doing it, and what defenses it worked best against.

Nowadays I see players around the league keeping fairly detailed notes about individuals they face, but I never did that. I didn't need notes to tell me about Darrell Green, the great cornerback for the Washington Redskins, because I knew everything I needed to know about him. Once you learn about what different players do, you just don't forget about it, especially as a quarterback. All you had to know about Darrell Green was if he was on the right, I was going to throw to the left. We were not going to try any trick plays against him, double moves, anything like that. The book on Darrell Green was simple: Stay away at all costs.

But I did keep a lot of general notes on plays and about philosophies on offense, and I had them everywhere in the house. Many times my wife would say, "Can I throw these playbooks and notepads away?" I'd say, "No, no, no." I kept them just in case I ever got the courage up to coach, so I could go back and look at some of those notepads and make use of some good ideas.

For years I'd walk by my closet and see hundreds of playbooks and notepads stacked on shelves. One day I finally said, "Who am I kidding? I'm not leaving broadcasting to go into coaching." And those playbooks and notepads went right into the garbage can.

The closest I ever came to becoming was coach was in 1995, after my first year in broadcasting with ESPN. Bill Belichick had approached me about coming back to play for the Cleveland Browns. My daughter, Deirdre, who was ten at the time, was especially excited about it. She had missed out on watching most of my career with the Giants and she wanted to see me play and be a part of it, if only for a brief period. In talking it over with my wife, we decided that if I did go back and play—whether it was for one year or two—I would do so with the objective that I would remain in football as a coach. I didn't know where or at what level that would be. I just knew that if I did reenter that world, I would never get out.

I ended up telling Bill, "Thanks, but no thanks."

It's different for coaches who decide to leave the sidelines to go into broadcasting or probably any other line of work. They can go back in the coaching profession and pick up right where they left off, at the height of their career. In the time they were away from the game they didn't lose that skill to coach like I lost the skill to be a player. If you told me I could go back and play again and have the same abilities and feelings that I had when I was thirty years old, I would toss aside the hair spray right now and go running back to the locker room again, because that was a tremendous time in my life.

That's a big part of the thought process behind the many coaching comebacks we have seen: Dick Vermeil, who burned out with the Eagles and then had a successful career broadcasting college football before winning a Super Bowl with St. Louis and moving on to try and win another with Kansas City; Bill Parcells, who also dabbled in television between coaching the Giants and Patriots and the Jets and Cowboys, and, more recently, Joe Gibbs, who is back on the sidelines in Washington, and Dennis Green, who did a little TV between his coaching stops in Minnesota and Arizona.

This is what Vermeil told me about his decision to come back to coaching after a fourteen-year absence: "When you're a leader of men, that's what you do. I believe that's what I am. That's what Bill Parcells is. That's why you get back in."

It's about the power of the position, the ability to control an organization, the challenge of trying to put together a team that has a chance to win, the feeling of exhilaration you get when it all comes together and you do win.

When Mike Ditka worked at CBS we sat together at dinner

one time, and I asked, "What was the better feeling, when you won the Super Bowl as a player with Dallas or when you won it as a coach with Chicago?"

"It wasn't even close," he said. "As a coach, it's much, much more satisfying."

"Really? I thought for sure you were going to say as a player."

"No, when you're a coach, there's just a special satisfaction you get from leading a team to victory, from putting it all together—the players, the coaches, the plays, the organization. Winning the Super Bowl as a coach was the greatest feeling that I ever experienced."

For me broadcasting is more than satisfying. I get a little bit of everything. I get to watch all the big games, which in itself makes it one of the greatest jobs on earth. I get to talk with the players and the coaches. And I get one of the best forums I could possibly have to talk to the fans about what I know and what I see on Sunday.

Yet, for someone who has been a head coach in the NFL, that isn't going to be nearly enough. There just isn't another business that can provide that sort of fulfillment. A coach's voice is the only one in his organization that counts each day. What he says is gospel. In broadcasting we answer to a lot of people. We're not the bosses. I would think that that would be pretty hard, if not impossible, for a former head coach in the NFL to get used to.

Now I realize that while Joe Gibbs was out of the NFL he was the boss of a highly successful NASCAR racing team. I don't know a whole lot about auto racing, but I have to wonder if the exhilaration from seeing your NASCAR team win a race is the same as seeing your National Football League team win a game. I guess the answer came when Joe walked away from the infield and returned to the football field. He had been out of the game and insisting that he would never come back, although I did hear him say he had thought about returning to coaching many times.

The draw was always there; he was just denying it publicly and maybe even to himself at times. Ever since I've known Joe Gibbs he has been a football guy. His passion, his deep love in life—besides his family—has to be football.

The lure of returning to the Redskins, whom he had once led to their greatest success, was just impossible for him to resist.

CHAPTER SIX

Learning and Living
the Parcells Way

"So what do you think, Simms? Are we going to
complete a pass today or, hell, am I going to have
another sleepless night? I need my rest."

—Bill Parcells

The way I do things in football—the way I do telecasts,
the way I talk about the game, the way I watch film—is
80 to 90 percent Bill Parcells. What else do I know? He had the
greatest influence on me as a player, and of course that will
never leave me.

When you read about Vince Lombardi and compare his style
with Bill Parcells's style, you see a lot of similarities. Beat 'em up
during the week. Love 'em just before the game. All through

practice it's, "You stink! You stink! You stink! Do better! Do better! Do better!" Then, right before the game, it's, "Hey, you guys are the best. You work hard. I think you're going to get it done. Just go play."

On game days Bill never put pressure on us. I never remember him giving us ultimatums or saying something that would make us tight or wouldn't make us confident about what we were doing. In fact, his other great saying on game day was, "Hey, remember, it isn't going to go perfect. Don't worry about it. This game is not about being perfect. Something's going to go wrong. Just keep going."

We were about to open the 1984 season against Philadelphia. Bill's pregame speech was over, and as I was walking out of the locker room I saw him standing at the door. He was about ten feet away, looking at me, and in a very upbeat voice he said, "All right, Simms. If you don't throw at least two interceptions today, that means you're not trying enough. I need plays. Make some daring plays. Go for the big plays. Don't be afraid."

My first thought was, *That's a weird thing to tell a quarterback right before a game.* However, the impact of what he said to me was amazing. It did exactly what he wanted. I'm not exaggerating when I say that it freed my mind. I just let it rip. We threw for more than 400 yards in our 28–27 win over the Eagles.

I'm not saying what Bill said was strictly the reason for that success, but, gosh, it did do a lot for me mentally. It just made me feel good, and more than anything it gave me room for error, knowing that it's not a perfect game.

When I think of how much he has meant to my career, not

only as a player but also as a broadcaster, it's hard to believe that we were ready to part ways with each other after he became the Giants' coach in 1983. I thought Bill's replacing Ray Perkins was one of the best things that could happen to me. I thought he was going to like me more as a quarterback than Scott Brunner just because I perceived myself to be a little more of a meat-and-potatoes guy.

I remember the day we both were going to meet with Parcells and he was going to tell us who the starter was. As I left that morning I told my wife, "It's going to be me. Don't even worry. I just can't imagine it going any other way."

I went down to the stadium, and as I headed into Parcells's office, Scott was coming out the door. I didn't even look at him to see if I could get a read from his face on Bill's decision. I walked in, sat down, and said, "Hey, Coach."

My butt didn't even hit the chair when he said, "Phil, I decided to go with Scott."

"Excuse me?" I said.

When he said it again, it didn't sound any more believable than the first time. In fact, I told him, "You've got to be kidding." He wasn't.

Looking back, I don't know if I judged my situation fairly. I thought I had played pretty well in the preseason. I was coming off a knee injury, but that wasn't a factor.

All I could come up with was that the decision had been preordained. I think Bill was going with Brunner all the way and there wasn't much I could do about it. The coaches just didn't trust me to do the right thing on the field once we started playing for keeps. They thought I was wild in everything I did—my actions, the way I handled myself. They just thought they were more secure with Scott Brunner. They just felt safer with him.

My initial reaction was just like that of any other spoiled athlete: "Trade me!"

"Is that what you want?" he said.

"Yeah, that's what I want."

"Well, I'll see what I can do about it."

What I've heard since was that George Young, the general manager, and Wellington Mara, the owner, didn't want to trade me. Guess what? I wasn't traded.

A few games into the season it wasn't going well with Scott, so Bill put me in against Philadelphia. I took us right down the field for a touchdown. The next time we got the ball we had a third-and-short, I dropped back to throw, and as my hand came down, it collided with one of the massive arms of defensive end Dennis Harrison. I felt extreme pain. I looked down and saw the bone was sticking right out of my thumb. I suffered a compound fracture of my right thumb. I was done for the year.

After a 3-12-1 finish the Giants got rid of Scott Brunner. Now I would have to beat out Jeff Rutledge, who started four games in '83, for the number one job in 1984. The Giants hired a strength coach, Johnny Parker, who became one of the dearest friends in my life. That off-season, thanks to a lot of badgering from me, Johnny agreed to put me on his lifting program for offensive linemen because he had yet to design one for the quarterbacks. I worked with less weight than the linemen did, but I followed the program religiously, to the point where Giants Stadium almost became my second home that spring.

My outlook was different. My personality was different. I

was much more professional in everything I did. After the second preseason game I was named the starter.

Bill could put all kinds of pressure on us before a practice. I remember one day in particular he did that in 1986, just as we were getting ready to walk out of the locker room. The practice the day before was not good. Bill didn't differentiate between a practice performance and a game—even if that game were the Super Bowl. He was not going to tolerate two poor practices in a row.

In a very angry tone he said to me, "Hey, are we going to complete a few f— passes today? Jesus Christ! I couldn't even sleep last night. I'm tossing and turning. My wife goes, 'What's the matter, Bill?' I said, 'What's the matter? My quarterback can't complete a pass, that's what's the matter. How in the hell am I going to win a game if my quarterback can't complete a pass?'

"So what do you think, Simms? Are we going to complete a pass today or, hell, am I going to have another sleepless night? I need my rest."

It hit me right in the face. I'll never forget it. On a scale of one to ten, for getting a verbal lashing from Bill, this was a good seven or eight. He drove his point home with a sledgehammer. My back actually tightened up from the stress.

Pat Hodgson, our wide receivers coach, happened to be standing right next to me at the time. He looked at me with a nervous smile and said, "I'm going to go warn those receivers it's coming fast and hard today."

We grow up with different kinds of fathers. There are those who will never hesitate to tell you when you've done a good job.

Then there is the kind of father that I had—the old-fashioned father for whom it took half his life just to say, "Hey, you did okay." He just wasn't into giving compliments. That was how he was raised and that was how he taught his kids. It was all about the work ethic he learned working on his dad's farm—which had corn, tobacco, sheep, cattle, hogs, and chickens—and later at the tobacco factory in Louisville where my mom also worked.

One night after coming home from a workout the summer before my freshman year of college, I took a shower, and as we sat down for dinner my father said, "You know, you sure have worked hard this summer. I'm proud of the way you've put your time in." I was spending my days at a full-time job at the Dr Pepper factory. After that I would work out, running and throwing. I also played baseball on the weekends. I knew I was working hard; I just never knew my father had noticed. When he acknowledged that, I thought, *Wow! That is like the greatest thing he has ever said to me.*

That's how Bill is, in a way. He puts you in a situation where, if he ever says, "You did a good job," you know it means so much more than that. It's a proud moment.

Everybody thinks he's just a curmudgeon and a mean man, but he definitely cares about his players as people. His approach wouldn't work if he didn't care. There were times in my career when I would struggle and he would just find the right moment and the right words, and say them to me.

In 1986, our first Super Bowl–winning season, we had games in which we couldn't even get 100 yards passing. One day, long after we had finished practice, I was the only one sitting in the locker room. It must have been about 7 o'clock at night when Bill came walking through, saw me sitting there, and sat down to talk with me.

"Look, you work hard," he said. "I know it's hard on you. It's not all your fault. Just keep doing what you're doing. Be fearless. Believe me, it'll work. It's gonna work."

He spoke in the same tone in which your father would speak to you at a particularly rough moment in your life. I felt a tremendous burden lifted off my shoulders. It took away the worry about messing up a play in a game.

In a key NFC showdown against Minnesota that year I completed a fourth-and-17 pass to Bobby Johnson, which set up the winning field goal in an emotional 22–20 victory. That probably was the biggest play of the season, because that win really catapulted us to our first Super Bowl.

Afterward Bill was outside of our locker room, chomping on a piece of gum as he spoke with the press. I was still in my uniform and, knowing I had to walk past him to get inside, I tried my best not to interrupt his news conference. But as I walked by Bill suddenly stopped talking. He pulled me aside, gave me a big hug, and actually planted a big kiss on my left cheek.

"You can play on my team anytime," he told me.

Then—as I found out years later when I finally watched a videotape of it for the first time—he told the reporters, "Any of you guys that think that guy can't play quarterback better start covering another sport, because he's pretty good."

Those situations are not common with him, but there are enough of them that happen to let everybody know that he does have a heart—that he can be very compassionate and humane. I think all the players on our team knew that side of him was always there. The question was, did you ever do anything to reach it?

As much as I would complicate the game sometimes Bill would break it down into simple, digestible little nuggets. He would say, "We're going to run it to the right. . . . We're going to throw it to the left. . . . We're going to throw three-step drops all week."

You'd say, "What? That's it?"

He'd say, "That's it."

One game in particular that comes to mind is when we went down to Washington and beat the Redskins with only a handful of plays. No kidding. You could have printed out the game plan on a cocktail napkin.

I had been getting killed in pass protection that year, so Bill said, "We're going to go with three-step drops and we're going to throw it quick. We'll split out one of our backs, so the safety has to cover him, and we'll throw three-step hitches, a slant, some hitch-and-gos, some out-and-ups."

That was our game plan. It doesn't get much simpler, which was why, going into the game, I was sweating bullets. I was convinced it was too simple. I was thinking, *We need 14 third-down plays, and we don't have them.* I felt underprepared, that we weren't clever enough to have a chance to win the game.

I felt even less comfortable when assistant coaches on our offensive staff actually came up to me during the week and said, "We can't win doing this. This is absurd."

Nevertheless, that was our plan. We carried it out. Quick

drops. Short throws. Some running here and there. I didn't get sacked. And we won.

As I walked off the field, Tom Coughlin, who was our wide receivers coach at the time, came up to me shaking his head.

"Unbelievable!" Tom said. "The man is unbelievable! How can you come into a game and do what we just did? It's just unbelievable!"

We really did more laughing than talking because it was something that defied words. We learned a huge lesson that day. Pick out one or two weaknesses of the other team, try to exploit them, and make sure they don't exploit your weaknesses. We couldn't pass-protect, so we didn't want to be dropping back and letting the Redskins exploit that with their strong defensive front. It ended up working to our favor.

It also told us a lot about Bill as a coach, how he perceived the game. Sometimes you shouldn't make it too complicated. Look for a little simple thing the opponent does, and just see if you can exploit the hell out of it. If you can, many times that's going to be enough to win the game.

Here's another Bill Parcells saying: "If you keep pressuring the other team and apply enough pressure to them, eventually they'll succumb to it." What that really means is play as hard as you can play, play smart, and just by doing that—never letting up and continuously coming out every round ready to battle and showing no signs of slowing down—sooner or later the other team will say, "They're never going to quit, so we might as well just get it over with and pack it in."

It used to be that you only heard about that sort of philosophy from a defensive perspective—that the defense would be relentless in its pursuit of the person with the ball or, if it was blitzing, it would keep coming and coming because the coaches on that side of the ball think the offense will just wilt under pressure sooner or later. Yet in the last five years I've heard more of that type of thinking shift to the offensive side.

Even announcers get into it, saying things like, "They keep pressuring you with speed down the field, throwing the ball down the field." Eventually, the defense can't take any more. You make a little mistake as a defensive back—you look the wrong way, you get overzealous trying to get over to a receiver when you shouldn't because that's not your responsibility in the particular coverage you're in—and you give up a big play. When the good teams apply pressure on you, you make the mistake first.

Why is Jerry Rice the greatest receiver ever to play the game? Because besides being immensely talented he's going to come out the very first play, run or pass, and do whatever he's doing full speed. Ten plays into the game, Jerry Rice is still doing it. Twenty plays. Thirty plays. It never, ever stops.

The defensive back covering him has to ask himself, "Can you match that same intensity?" Almost always, the answer is no. There will be one time in the game when that defensive back will say, *Whew! Let's just take a little breather here.* And that's when Jerry Rice is going to make the big play to win the game. He will outlast you. He will outwork you. His motivation and desire never waver.

You've got to practice what you want to preach, and our practices with the Giants were always under pressure. Even though it was practice you had to do everything you did as if it were a game. There was always a great sense of urgency because you can't do it in a game unless you do it in practice.

In the preseason Bill would always make sure to take us to a place on the road where the stadium would be packed and much louder and more enthusiastic than you would ever imagine in August. Green Bay was one of the spots; Bill always loved to take us up there. Lambeau Field in the preseason was just like a regular-season game. The stands were full. The crowd was loud. It was as tough an atmosphere as a visiting team could experience in the preseason. You got a great taste of everything you're going to face on the road when the regular season came around: lots of noise, lots of adversity, and lots of pressure from the fans and your own coaches.

I had to laugh in the summer of 2003 when Coach Parcells, in his third preseason game after returning to coaching with Dallas, had the Cowboys play in Pittsburgh. It was a packed house at Heinz Field. A lot of noise. A lot of emotion. Everything that he wanted his players to experience in the preseason. Reading quotes from Bill in Texas newspapers before and after the game, I felt as if I had gone back in time. Before the game, he said, "I like going to Pittsburgh and Green Bay in the preseason because I think they're the closest things to regular-season games that you can get. I told (the players) I thought Pittsburgh was a good place to play because it's kind of a raucous place."

After the Cowboys' 15–14 loss to the Steelers, Bill said, "I would have liked to come in here and try to convince this team that they could win on the road. They have not been doing that very well, and this could have given them some confidence . . . but we fell short."

The feelings I had were the same that I felt a couple of months later when I picked up one of the New York papers and saw an article on Quincy Carter, the Cowboys' former quarter-back. It talked about how he was watching film of their home games at the team complex only hours after the final gun because that would give him a jump in his preparation for the next game.

Bill even had him saying all the right things. I watched Quincy in a television interview, and no matter what the question was, he basically said nothing: "Yeah, we're working hard. . . . We're trying our best. . . . We're trying to get better. . . . We're trying to get rid of mistakes. . . . We're just trying to do what the coaches tell you to do." It made you think back to the sage advice Kevin Costner gave Tim Robbins in the movie *Bull Durham*: "Learn your clichés. Study them. Know them. They're your friends."

I feel a bond with every quarterback who has ever played for Coach Parcells. He has such high expectations for his quarter-back. He wants him to be the hardest worker and the commander on the field. He wants him to get the offense in the end zone. He wants him to be able to respond well to pressure.

Every successful coach or businessman, whatever we are in life, is always thinking and always planning. That was exactly what Bill Parcells was doing one day in the summer of 1988 as I walked to the practice field during training camp. It was about a 250-yard walk to the field. I still had a few minutes to get there, but I was walking pretty fast.

As I looked up, about 20 yards ahead of me, there was Bill. I was hustling to get to the field on time, but I didn't want to have to walk by Coach Parcells because you never could just walk by him. If you did you usually were going to get some pretty cutting comments thrown your way. Finally, I got up the courage and just decided I would try and walk as fast as I could and hope that Bill might let me off the hook for a change.

But as I tried to speed past him, he said, "Hey, boy!"

"Hey, Coach," I said. "I've got to go. I've got to get up to the practice field."

"Slow down, slow down. It's okay if you're late. You're with me."

"Okay, Coach. How's it going?"

"Hey, I want you to know, Phil, that I'm really proud of you. You're having a tremendous training camp. You're working hard. You're playing well. I just couldn't be prouder of you."

Here I was bracing myself for the worst, and I ended up saying, "Thanks, Coach."

"Sure," he said. "But before you go, I just want you to know that sometime during practice today I am going to jump your ass."

I couldn't believe my ears.

"What do you mean you're going to jump my ass?" I said. "How do you know if I'm going to do something wrong?"

"Oh, it doesn't matter. Something will come up during practice. But I've got to jump your ass today because I want the rest of those guys up there to see that if I can jump my quarterback and get all over you, it's okay if I yell at them and get all over them, too. Just take it the right way. Don't get upset. Don't pout."

What do you say to that?

Practice started, and it went along as a normal, training-camp practice. About an hour and a half into it I threw an incompletion and Bill threw a temper fit right in the middle of the field.

"What are you doing?" he yelled. "How could you do that?"

It was not a full-out, killer yell, but it was a good one. The fans thought it was funny. The rest of the players all stopped to listen. I was embarrassed. Of course, any time the head coach yells at the quarterback, it brings snickers from the rest of the group. The other players are glad it's not them, but they're even happier to see that it's the guy who's perceived as being untouchable sometimes. Bill got rid of that myth really quick. He proved his point. Yelling at me served its purpose.

That's a normal happening at a Bill Parcells practice. But once it's over, you just move on and go forward. You can't sit around and sulk or have, as Bill would say, a "brook trout look on your face." You've just got to get out there and perform. Bill's yelling is just part of the pressure, part of the life of being around him when you're a player and he's the coach. When I was with the Giants, it didn't happen every day. But in training camp, he'd have a good one about once every three days. It wasn't a big deal. Bill also knew that if he yelled at me, I could handle it well enough to continue practice.

Anybody was fair game. Well, almost anybody. There were exceptions. I don't ever remember if Bill really called out Lawrence Taylor on the practice field. He might give him a comment every now and then to spur him on, but nothing that was out of control and loud like he would do to the rest of us. For one, everybody on the team knew that Lawrence was "The

Man" on the team and that he was just under a different set of rules than us. Two, Lawrence was such a great player Bill didn't have a reason to get on him in practice too often.

Paul Tagliabue, the commissioner of the NFL, once told me a story about when, during a Jets training-camp practice, he was talking with Bill at the middle of the field. All of a sudden, Bill said, "Excuse me, just for one minute here, Commissioner." He turned, looked all the way down at the end zone, picked out one of his prominent defensive backs, and began yelling at him, "You'd better start doing things right. . . . I don't want to see any more mistakes out here." He turned back to resume his conversation with the commissioner, who said, "That's unbelievable. You were talking to me, but you could still see that he was doing something wrong all the way on the other end of the field?"

"I didn't see what he was doing," Bill said. "I just wanted to yell at him. I knew I was going to yell at him at some point in practice, and I just picked my spot to yell at him now."

It sent a message. It served a purpose. After that the rest of the players are thinking, *Coach is always watching us. We'd better make sure we're doing it right all the time.*

Your philosophical beliefs determine whether you win or lose. What you believe in, deep down, as a coach and as an organization, forms and becomes your team. How you dress it up with some of your X's and O's and all the cute stuff is the final piece that really gets you over the top to win. However, what you believe in—great physical conditioning, toughness, practicing under pressure—forms the core, because that's how you're going to play.

There has to be a master plan. You're not going to go out on the field on Sunday and be overly aggressive and the roughest and toughest bunch out there if you don't work on it in practice. No coach can go through a week where it's always easy, and then all of a sudden say, "All right, men, let's turn it on."

Playing aggressively and having that edge is a deep-seated mentality that you can only develop over a long period of time and through constant reinforcement. It's something you just can't create overnight. It's something you have to learn to accept.

For the Giants, we started to learn this in 1984, but it didn't all come to fruition until 1986, when we won the Super Bowl. It took three seasons of a lot of yelling and a lot of work. It took coaches stressing the little things, over and over, such as showing a linebacker the proper technique to stop a tight end from blocking him.

I tell people all the time that the hardest part of playing under that coaching staff wasn't Bill Parcells. It was his assistants: Al Groh, Bill Belichick, Romeo Crennel, Mike Pope, Ron Erhardt. They were all vocal. They were all rough. They all could generate some fear. Ron Erhardt, man, he was old school. He would call your ass out on the field. He would call your ass out in the meeting room in front of the whole team.

Establishing a foundation is the hardest thing for coaches to do. But once you establish what you are, what your team is, what you're going to be as an organization, the reinforcement kind of takes care of itself. When the newcomers arrive, the coach doesn't have to sit down and teach them everything because he knows his incumbent players and his organization are going to mold them. You learn quickly what is accepted and not accepted. The coach doesn't even have to give the newcomers his agenda-setting speech because his other players are going to snap them into shape. They tell them, "For this to work right, for us to win, you've got to get in line with the rest of us."

Everybody needs disciples. You've got to have people help you spread your message. You teach the whole group, but really you need the core guys, the ones making a lot of plays for you, to sell your ideas to everybody else.

I also believe you have to treat all of your players differently. You can't have a steadfast rule that's going to hold true for every single person on the team because some people respond well to being yelled at while some people respond much better to being patted on the back. And, with some, there has to be a mixture. You just have to figure it out and do it the right way.

When I was with the Giants I remember we had a left tackle, Brad Benson, whom the coaches yelled at relentlessly and brutally. We had a center, Bart Oates, whom the coaches yelled at relentlessly and brutally. Why? Because they could take it. They responded favorably to it. Yelling at them would just make them more determined to perform at the highest level they could. They would say, "All right, I'll show you!"

We also had a left guard, Billy Ard, who played his best if you simply didn't ever say anything to him. You just had to leave him alone. If you yelled at Billy he would say, "All right, I'll show you . . . I just won't do anything." It was the same with our right guard, Chris Godfrey, so you had to be very kind to him, too.

Lawrence Taylor could respond to anything. If you loved

him, he'd respond. If you hated him, he'd respond. Of course, Bill didn't pick on Lawrence much because it rarely was necessary. Over my career I want to say he did it maybe three, four, five times to Lawrence. If Lawrence happened to be in one of his occasional slumps, Bill would yell, "Lawrence! I don't know. We're just going to have to change your name to 'What's the matter with . . .' Because all I ever hear from everybody is, 'What's the matter with Lawrence? What's the matter with Lawrence?' I don't know what to tell them."

Bill would just egg him on, knowing that that would get to Lawrence. You have to remember, Lawrence was like a quarterback. Media and fans expected him to deliver the defensive equivalent of touchdown passes—taking the ball away from opponents, scoring himself or putting us in scoring position—on a fairly regular basis. When he didn't deliver he was going to hear about it. And when Bill picked those rare moments to call him out, Lawrence would respond. One of those times was a game in '86, down in Washington, when I think he sacked Jay Schroeder something like six times to help us to a big win. It just seemed every time Lawrence hit him it was a sack, a fumble, or both.

Bill's always looking for your hot button, whatever it takes to get to you. There are a lot of buttons for him to push. The most important is always the one that makes you play better. And he'll always find it. He knew what my hot button was before I knew it. He figured me out before I figured myself out. That's one of his gifts.

For me that button was never allowing me to feel satisfied, and Bill never pushed it harder than he did after a 1988 game against the Detroit Lions in Giants Stadium. We had had a slim lead at halftime, during which Bill rode us pretty hard, which was uncommon because he wasn't much of a yeller at halftime regardless of the score. I went out in the second half and played extremely well. We won big. I had such a strong game I actually couldn't wait to watch the film the following day.

After I saw that film my performance looked better than I even imagined. I threw three deep passes that were on the mark and real backbreakers for the Lions. I made good decisions. I took advantage of some fine coaching points that had been made to me during the week.

At the end of the day—after meetings, working out, and receiving treatment—I was sitting at my locker and feeling just awesome. I was looking forward to going home and having one of the great dinners that my wife always prepared for me on Mondays. I was going to eat, kick back in the TV room, and watch *Monday Night Football*. Life just doesn't get any better than that for the quarterback of a professional football team.

Or so I thought.

Just as I was about to go out the door Coach Parcells happened to walk through the locker room. He saw me and said, "Son, you did pretty good yesterday." Even as the words were coming out of my mouth, I was thinking, *I shouldn't even dare say this, but what the hell?*

"Ah, come on, Coach," I said. "I was great yesterday."

Bill stood there and looked at the ground for what seemed like forever as I awaited his response. Then he looked up at me, shook his head, and said, "Son, it disappoints me to think that my expectations for you are greater than the ones that you have for yourself."

It crushed me. It floored me. For as high as I had been, now I was lower than I could possibly get. And what made it worse was that he walked away from me before I could even think of a response.

I got in my car and all I could think about the whole drive home was, *I'll show that damn coach that my expectations for myself are extremely high.*

Looking back, I realize that I fell right into the trap that he had set. Even though I truly couldn't have played any better, Bill didn't want me to believe it. He wanted me to keep striving to improve and reach new heights.

CHAPTER SEVEN

There's Only One Cure for Cabin Fever: Take Your Hits and Come Back for More

"My God! That game! I just didn't realize how rough it is!"

—Diana Simms

As I walk through airports or sit in restaurants, people always come up to me and ask, "Do you miss playing?"

"No," I say. "It took a while, but I'm over it."

Invariably the next thing they'll say is, "Yeah, but I bet you don't miss taking all those hits and waking up the morning after games all beat up and sore."

My answer always catches them by surprise: "Actually, I do miss that." And I'm not saying that merely because I took too many hits to the head. I kind of liked waking up the morning after games all beat up and sore. It was positive feedback for what I did for a living. It felt good to roll over in bed and sit up and move around and look at all the bumps and bruises on my body and know, *I took their best shot and we still won the game*. It felt natural.

In football being hit is part of your working conditions. Once you're used to it, it's not a problem. It's like getting up at four o'clock in the morning to go to work. That's tough to do if you had been waking up at eight every morning. Getting up four hours earlier kicks your butt until you get used to it.

People who look at pro football and see the speed, the power, and the hitting are going from zero contact to the most physical sport in the world at its highest level. You have to re-member that most professional football players have experi-enced contact over an extended period from recreational league to middle school to high school to college and, finally, to the pros. The intensity of the hitting increases so gradually along the way that a lot of times you don't even notice it, so the pun-ishment you take is not as bad as the general public perceives it when you think about it in those terms.

This is one way to illustrate it: I walk into an office, pick out a healthy businessman in his early twenties, and gently tap him on the back of his head. Each day over ten years I gradually in-crease the intensity of that tap. By the end of that ten-year span I'll be able to rear back and slap that businessman as hard as possible and it won't bother him. It will be a big deal to everyone else in that office who sees it and hears it, but it won't be such a big deal to the businessman who is now in his early thirties because he has become conditioned to absorb the hit and not let it affect his workday.

Isn't it amazing that a major-league baseball player can swing and hit that 95 mph fastball? Remember, they've been training to do that their whole lives. They started at tee ball. Then their fathers pitched underhanded to them. Then they were ten years old and they pitched to each other and the ball was coming in at 50 mph. Over time that speed gradually increased to the point where a baseball traveling toward them at 90 mph became a normal part of their working environment.

I think you figure out at an early age—which is when most players start playing football—either you like the contact or you don't. A lot of young men like the contact. It's the ultimate macho thing for men. It's testing your manhood, what you're made of.

I think that's what makes football so exciting on TV, too—it's extremely physical and it's fast. For men, it's everything they would want to do if they could. For women, I don't think it's a stretch to say that seeing two men hitting each other is at least part of the game's allure.

Sometimes as a player you wear the hitting and the physical part of it as a badge of honor. You deliver the hits. You absorb them. You don't complain and you keep on going.

Other players admire you for it. They talk to each other about it. You get a reputation for your ability to take a hit. It becomes who you are in the eyes of everyone throughout the league. I remember how much I would be commended for it.

Someone would say, "Hey, you stood in there, you took the hits, and you still threw it." My answer was, "Yeah, I did. I want to succeed. That's the only way I know I'm going to succeed, so I have to do it that way." If I didn't do that I wouldn't have been playing.

You play without fear. You play with smarts, but you play without fear. You never worry about getting hit. You never worry about getting hurt. I think all players are like that. Once you start to think that you don't want to get hit, a lot of times that's when your career's in trouble. Because when you start thinking about cutting down hits, it's going to affect your judgment as a player.

Bill Parcells used to say, "Once you develop cabin fever as a quarterback, then it's over." Cabin fever is when you get a little claustrophobic as you drop back because there are a lot of people around you, and you think about not wanting to take that punishment. It's a quarterback who gets antsy, who moves before he should, who throws the ball away a little before he should, who isn't seeing down the field as clearly as he should. Cabin fever is a disease and it is terminal for a quarterback in the National Football League.

When you drop back you have to be free of mind. You can't be worried about taking punishment. Once you're cognizant that things are tight and it's dicey, then it's over. The pocket does get tight. People are right next to you, but you have to act like they're not there.

A bunch of quick thoughts enter a quarterback's mind as he sees a receiver. He knows a defender is right near him. He knows what he's trying to accomplish. He knows the ramifications. And he tries to judge it: Is it worth the hit? All these thoughts happen in the time it takes to snap your fingers. Almost always, the quarterback is going to go ahead and take the punishment, make the throw, and hope to survive.

A lot of that comes from knowing how to take the hit. You relax rather than tense up because when you relax you absorb the impact rather than allowing it to jolt you.

One of the best feelings of all for a quarterback is to throw the ball, take a big hit, and put the pass exactly where you want it for the completion. The defender hits you and he's so proud that he has really laid it on you—that he has crushed you. He is the biggest, baddest man in the world. That's what's going on in his head.

Then he realizes that you don't have the ball. Then he realizes you've completed a 20-yard throw. You sense the frustration he's feeling from the words that come out of his mouth, from his body language, or from that little shove he gives you as he is getting up. That's one of the best feelings there is for a quarterback. It's all the circumstances you could want in one play.

Of course, the tables can turn very quickly. We were playing the St. Louis Cardinals and Al "Bubba" Baker, their star defensive end at the time, flushed me on three plays during the opening drive. All three times I hit the receiver for big gains as we marched 80 yards down the field. Finally, I hit our tight end, Zeke Mowatt, on a little move-go pattern where he ran straight for 8 yards, broke to the sideline for 3 yards and then turned back upfield in the right seam for a touchdown. All Al could do was yell, "Dang!" I couldn't resist the chance to rub it in a little.

"I am hot today, big boy!" I said.

Al didn't respond.

As the game proceeded and Al continued to hit me, the tide kind of turned. All of a sudden we were losing, 31–21. It was getting late in the game. I threw the ball, he hit me, the pass fell incomplete.

"Now how hot are you, big boy?" Al said. He stuffed it right back in my face. I deserved it. I just shut up and took my medicine on the way to a loss.

The greatest trash-talker I ever faced was Charles Haley. During a *Monday Night Football* game against San Francisco, when the 49ers were terrific on defense, Haley came out of nowhere to hit me twice as I was throwing. Both times the ball flew up in the air, and both times O. J. Anderson picked it up and ran for about 10 yards. I think those were our longest gains of the night. After the second hit Charles just stopped on his way back to the huddle and whispered in my ear. I can't repeat exactly what he said, but let's just say it was a warning that if I kept dropping back to pass he was going to do a little more than just knock me to the ground.

Normally, whenever a defensive player said something derogatory to me I would come back with something like, "Shove it!" But when Charles said what he said, in that menacing lisp of his, I wasn't thinking that it was just mere trash talk. I was thinking, *He means it.* It was frightening. One reason a comment like that carried so much weight from Charles was that he was such an unbelievable pass rusher. He was one of those guys that, as you dropped back, you always had to have a feel for where he was and whether he was going to blow the play up. Fortunately I survived to tell the story in these pages.

• • •

When I played I never thought that much about how my being hit affected my family—my mom and dad, my wife, and my kids when they were younger. I only thought about it when I quit. I started watching my sons play, and I thought, *Oh, my poor mom and dad. They went through a lot—to have to suffer through watching you play and all the goods and bads and the injuries.* In fact, I told my mother, "God, Mom, I just didn't realize what I was putting you through in your life."

"Oh, I know," she said. "It's a lot of years, and you live and die with every game. You worry about injury. You worry about success and failure, and it's tough."

At most games my wife, Diana, usually sat in the mezzanine section or far back in the lower section. But one night late in my career, when she took my oldest son, Christopher, and about six or seven of his friends from the neighborhood to a preseason game against the Jets, I was able to get them front-row tickets right behind our bench. I just thought it would be a little more fun for them to be closer to the action and I could turn around and say hi to them or give them the thumbs-up.

At the time the Jets' game was THE preseason game in New York. It was big. It was emotional. We approached it as if it counted. We game-planned. Starters played at least three quarters, sometimes even more. It was like the real thing. And it was brutal. It was just rough.

It was the era when the Jets had Mark Gastineau, Joe Klecko, Marty Lyons, and our team was pretty good. It was a tremendous game. It was as hard-hitting as any game you could see. It was physical for me. I played extremely well and we won.

As I walked into our front door at home I was expecting to hear my wife say, "Wow! Great game! It was fun!" When you opened our front door, you could see down a hallway into our kitchen. As soon as I pulled the door open my wife spotted me. She had this wide-eyed look and came running toward me, yelling, "Phil!!!" I was taken aback, wondering why she was so exasperated.

"My God! That game!" she said. "I just didn't realize how rough it is!"

That was because, for every previous game she had seen me play for the Giants in person, she had always been about 75 yards from the field. On that night she was 15 yards away. For the first time she could get a true sense of how much hitting there was and how hard it was. It caught her off guard.

"My God!" she said. "It's so rough! It's so tough! I can't believe it!"

It started to get to me a little because I had never thought about it in those terms. I started thinking that she was so concerned for my welfare, that the thought of my taking that kind of punishment was just too much for her and she wanted me to retire.

"I'm sorry, dear," I said. "Let's wait until the year is over, then we'll sit down and if you think I should retire we'll talk about it."

"Oh, no, you're not quitting," she said. "You're going to play at least until you're forty. Then we'll talk about you retiring. I'm just talking about my kids. I'm not letting them get into this sport."

Here we are now, fifteen years later, and I have one son,

Christopher, playing quarterback for the Tampa Bay Bucca-neers and another, Matthew, who is a high school quarterback.

When you stop playing, you're changing from—for lack of a better term—a violent life to a normal life. There's no in be-tween. After I retired I would say, "I'd like to play again, but, God, I don't want to get hit anymore. It's over. It was cool when I was playing, but no more."

If there were any doubts about that, they disappeared in late February 2004. That was when Christopher and Matthew sat down one night at our home in New Jersey to watch some tapes of my old games. I sat down and watched with them. After about ten minutes of seeing myself pounded repeatedly by the Eagles I began to wince. It hurt more to witness those hits on a TV screen than to actually be hit in the game because I am so unconditioned to even think about taking punishment and being beat up and sore. Sometimes it's even hard to believe I did it back then.

After the coach, the person who has the chance to wield the second-greatest amount of power on a football team is the quarterback. Unless there is a player at another position who just has extraordinary talent (Ray Lewis, Baltimore's All-World linebacker and incredibly powerful leader, is a good example), there is no one else who has more influence on his team's for-tunes than the guy handling the ball all the time.

Everything he does—his work habits, how he practices, how he plays, how he conducts himself—sets the mood and agenda for the whole team. It's knowing when to cut up with the rest of the players and when to be serious. You can't always be quite "one of the guys," but sometimes you can be close. It's almost like a head coach giving the players the human touch while staying aloof enough to remind everyone who's in charge.

Can you measure the importance of that? No. The coaches see it, though. You're bringing something out there besides just doing your job. It's not a quality you need to be a Super Bowl quarterback, because players who have the personalities of rocks have achieved that. But it helps.

A quarterback also has got to be a tireless worker. Some of those other players might be cutting up and doing their thing, but they want to know that their quarterback is in that back room studying film and working. And, by God, he'd better be. That's what they want him to be doing, because they know that that's important to their team's chances for success. You are making players around you better because you demand they work along with you. If you're a hard worker, you're leaving the rest of the guys on the team no choice. They have to work at the same speed you are to stay with you. Otherwise, they'll look lazy.

As a quarterback you've got to come to work with a certain amount of energy every day. Joe Gibbs once said to me about his quarterback-turned-announcer, Joe Theismann, "Whatever you think about Joe, whatever you say about him, the one thing I never had to worry about was our team having so-so practices, because Joe Theismann is hyper. He loved to practice. So every day, he would come out to practice and say, 'Hey, let's go! Let's go! Yeah! Yeah! Yeah!'"

That brought enthusiasm. It raised the energy level at practice, and when you do that, guys pay attention. They work harder. Those are the types of things that make you a better football team on Sunday. A quarterback is capable of having that kind of influence on the rest of his team.

There are exceptions—guys that are so extraordinary at what they do at another position, they can inspire and lift everyone else, too. Lawrence Taylor could do that for us. If Lawrence came out and decided he was going to rip it up at practice, man, practice took on a whole new meaning and whole new energy level.

Quarterbacks can put pressure on coaches, too. All it takes is making a little bit of a pest of yourself, saying, "Hey, Coach, why don't we do more? Let's do this. Let's do that." Now the coach feels challenged to come up with more plays to keep pace with his quarterback.

I can't remember the year—it might have been 1988—but I was getting hit quite a bit. We were doing okay, but I was getting hit more than I should have been for a good-quality football team, which we were at that point. Our practices were pretty close to the real thing, so even though the quarterback was supposed to be off limits as far as contact, the defense was allowed to rush and get in my way. One day we were practicing kind of sloppy. I couldn't throw because I was getting pushed around, and Bill Parcells had seen enough. He stopped the practice. He was really pissed off.

"Damn this offensive line!" he yelled. "My quarterback's back here, taking beatings in games. Hell, we can't even practice. Guys are all over him. You're going to get him hurt. Then what are we going to do?"

I was standing right behind him, and I was thinking, *Yeah, good, Bill. Rip their ass because they're not protecting me the way they should.* Bill went on and on, seemingly forever. Then he stopped. He turned around to look at me.

"And you know what, Simms?" Bill said. "It's all your damn fault."

My mouth dropped. It felt as if all the blood fell right out of my body. All I could think was, *What the hell is he talking about?*

Parcells wasn't finished.

"You see all these guys up here?" Bill said, pointing to the offensive linemen. "You used to be their leader. They used to fear you. They were afraid for their guy to hit you because they knew you'd jump their ass. But no. Now you're their little buddy. *Buddy, buddy, buddy. Take us out to dinner, Phil.*

"Yeah, take them out to dinner. Spoil their damn ass. Don't be a leader anymore. No wonder they don't protect you."

All I could think was, *Wow!*

We finished practice. I got in my car, and I still didn't quite grasp what had happened. I was driving home and I was thinking about why I had gotten chewed out—one more time—on the field. The more I thought about it, the more I thought Bill was right. Being the quarterback brings a status with it. It brings power, and I wasn't using that power anymore. I lost it just by becoming one of the guys.

It was probably inevitable. One, we're human; it's just a natural instinct to bond a little more. Two, we had been together for a long time. Three, we had success. Through the years you also lose a little bit of that edge it takes to be extremely successful. You just kind of get tired. You just kind of say, "Let's have a good time."

It's okay to separate yourself from them a little because that's what you have to do. No matter how much the head coach talked to me—whether it was Ray Perkins, Bill Parcells, Ray Handley, or Dan Reeves—I never lost sight of the fact that this was the man with the power regardless of what I said to him or what the conversation was about. Even if Bill Parcells became personable—even if he was having fun or asking my opinion or we were talking about something besides football— no matter what he said or did, when he talked to me, there was always that little voice telling me, "Be careful! This is THE MAN you're talking to here."

But I let that line between me and my offensive linemen get crossed. I didn't do it consciously. It just happened. I kind of let my personal and professional relationships with those guys blend together. All of a sudden there was no separation anymore. They were still my friends, of course, but that separation had to be there. Parcells always used to say, "Hey, Simms, I don't need a cruise director. I need a battleship commander."

Can you define it any better than that? He wanted me to be him out there. He couldn't play quarterback, so I had to do it for him and bring his personality to the huddle. It was an awesome feeling to have somebody expect that of you and think that you could do it—be his commander.

"Take control of that huddle," Bill would say. "Nobody talks in that huddle but you. You are in charge of what's going on. And when you call a play, by God, call it with meaning. Say it strongly. Say it forcefully. Make them believe that that play you're gonna call is gonna work."

I was able to regain that commander's status by just conducting myself the right way, which meant letting everyone else on the offense know that I was running the ship, I was the general on the field. The things that I would say to these superlarge human beings during games were incredible. I would say terrible things, and they would take it.

Bart Oates was my center, and I always picked on him. We'd come to the sidelines, and I'd yell, "Bart!"

He'd run over to me like a little kid and go, "Yeah? Yeah? Yeah?"

I'd start screaming, "What the hell's going on? I'm getting hit all the time. That's bullshit! Goddang it! Go straighten it out! That better not happen again." I would just be beside myself.

And Bart would say, "Okay! Okay! I'll get it straightened out. I'll get it fixed up."

That was how I communicated with my offensive linemen most of the time—I'd yell at Bart. He would say things to me during a game, and I'd go, "Oh, shut up! I'm the one calling the plays! You get in the huddle and shut up!"

"Okay."

We were playing the Cowboys in our final regular-season game in 1993. The winner was going to get home-field advantage through the play-offs. In my eyes it was going to determine who was going to win the Super Bowl, because I knew we were going to get the week off and whomever we played was going to come into the Meadowlands, where it gets cold and windy that time of year. We were awesome in those situations. No one even wanted to deal with us. But I knew if we lost the game and had to go on the road, we would have no chance.

All of a sudden I found out that Jumbo Elliott, my left tackle who was blocking Charles Haley that day, wouldn't be playing in the overtime period. He was out because of a sore back.

"What?" I yelled. "Where is he?"

I walked over to Jumbo, who was lying on the ground in front of our bench. He was moaning and groaning in agony.

"Jumbo, what's up?" I said.

"Oh, man, my back," he said.

"Jumbo, we have got to have you. We have no chance if you're not in the game. You've got to play, man. I'm sorry. You've got to get up. You've got to get the f— up! Now!"

And it was like I blessed him with my hand. He rolled over. As he did, he let out a "Ohhhh! Ohhhh!" Finally, he stood up and let out another, "Ohhhhhh!" He just kept making all these noises, and the rest of us were saying, "Ah, he's all right. He's going in."

Sure enough, the sonofagun went out there, half-crippled, and blocked Charles Haley for that overtime. He blocked him well, too, even though we still lost, 16–13. It was unbelievable.

Now that my career's over, I wonder, *Why didn't he just take me and slam me to the turf and it would have been over?* But never did I have one of the offensive linemen stand up to me and say, "If you say one more word about me, I'm going to kick your ass right here." Or, "I'm going to meet you after practice and kick your ass."

What stopped any of those guys from just decking me? The title. You don't screw with the quarterback as long as he doesn't put himself in a position where you can screw with him.

Offensive linemen also have to suppress their ego, which

seems to come naturally to them. They seem to be very happy working in a group. And, of course, when NFL teams do the IQ testing before the draft, they're the smartest group on the field. They generally score higher than quarterbacks do. I guess you've got to be somewhat of a deep thinker to work and to go unnoticed and to take all of that abuse and not let it bother you.

From the teams I cover on a regular basis for CBS, one of the best leaders I see among the quarterbacks is Tom Brady. He has a certain way about him. The players like him. They respect him because he works, he plays hard, and he plays well. He's one of the guys sometimes, but he's not always one of the guys. He uses his power effectively.

Peyton Manning does it very well, too. The difference with Manning and the others is that he is such a high-profile player. He couldn't lay low if he tried. The American public's not going to let him, TV's not going to let him, and the reporters are not going to let him. But that leadership is in him. He was born with it.

Donovan McNabb shows it, too. He has a little something about him, a little of that Pied Piper in him. People want to follow him. He conducts himself in the right way at all times. He doesn't do anything around the team or in public that would ever disgrace himself as a professional athlete or as a professional football player or as a quarterback.

Add Steve McNair to that list, too. He received maybe the nicest compliment I ever heard a player give one of his teammates. It was 1997, and the Tennessee Titans were in Dallas on Thanksgiving Day. We interviewed Bruce Matthews, the Titans' perennial Pro Bowl offensive lineman, the night before the game. I asked him a question about Steve McNair, and he said, "You know, I only have one regret."

"What's that?" I asked.

"That I'm not going to be able to play for another ten years, because I'd like to be able to stay in that huddle with Steve McNair. He is really a special guy."

For an older guy who had been to the Pro Bowl at every offensive line position to say that about a young quarterback is pretty remarkable. That just says it all about the power of the quarterback.

CHAPTER EIGHT

Knowing the Difference Between Good and Great

Very seldom do I ever say the word *great* during a telecast. It goes back to what I learned from Bill Parcells—that the word *great* is thrown out there way too often by media, fans, coaches, players, everybody.

A great player is someone who does extraordinary things, who plays above the ability of the people he's competing against or are around him and does it for a long period of time. It's something that holds true in all sports. Michael Jordan was born with great athletic ability. He worked hard to enhance his ability, but then he had the desire, the natural intelligence, and basketball smarts to push all of it to the limit. That's greatness and it's not found in very many athletes.

When I was with the Giants, early in the morning before home games, two of our offensive linemen, Karl Nelson and Brad Benson, running back Maurice Carthon, wide receiver Phil McConkey and me would pull up chairs with Coach Parcells in the middle of the locker room. We'd sit around for about a half-hour, drinking coffee, and talk about different topics—the game we were about to play, stuff that happened in practice, the previous week's game, the previous day's college football games. Many of our discussions also focused on which players in the league we thought were truly great.

Bill would ask, "How many great players do you think there are in the NFL?"

"Oh, there's about fifty," I'd say.

"Fifty? You can't name me five."

I'd name a guy. Bill would look at me as if I were nuts and say, "Are you kidding me? He's not great. The league's full of people like him. This guy's only had one good year. Talk to me after he's had five straight good years."

Every time we'd offer a name he'd shoot it down.

"Nope! Hasn't done it long enough."

"Nope! He's a one-year wonder."

It was amazing. We couldn't even get to five because Bill's criteria were extremely harsh. To this day, I still think about that when I judge players and talk about them on the air.

Great becomes almost a crutch that announcers use. It was a veteran announcer, Marv Albert, who told me just as I was getting ready to go into broadcasting, "Don't get in the habit of saying everything's great. 'Great guy . . . great coach . . . great play . . . great call . . . great catch,' because it diminishes what the word should stand for." As soon as he said that I thought back to those conversations with Bill. When I say "great," I want it to be something special—about a special circumstance or a special player.

The two greatest football players I've ever seen are Jim Brown and Lawrence Taylor. As a young kid growing up in Louisville, where the Browns were on TV every week, I saw a lot of Jim Brown. Maybe it was just because I was a kid, but even at a young age I could see that Jim Brown looked physically superior to everyone else on the field.

From what I saw in person, I can't think of another player that compares with Lawrence Taylor. My gosh! Even if you knew nothing about football, you could see that he was different from anybody else you had ever practiced or played with. He had skill that was unique and new to the NFL. In 1981, when he came into the league, linebackers were not as fast or as agile as Lawrence.

Before he came into the league running backs used to be able to block outside linebackers on the pass rush. But it was evident early on that running backs, who were giving up so much size and strength, had no chance of blocking Lawrence one-on-one in passing situations. Teams had to change the way they designed pass blocking against the Giants. They had to find ways to get the much larger offensive linemen to block Lawrence Taylor. When you played us, you actually had to change your offensive philosophy, just because you had to find a different way to deal with him. Anytime a player can force an opponent to change its fundamental way of doing things, that's a sign that that player is great.

It's just like, in baseball, when Barry Bonds comes to the plate, his team may be losing 3–1, with men on first and second and two outs. What does the opposing team do? It walks him, even though it is putting the tying run in scoring position on second base. That's the ultimate sign of respect for a great hitter.

Lawrence had tremendous skill and, man, did he like to play the game. For him, there was nothing better than the battle—the chance to get after it, to beat the guy across from him. Lawrence was a ferocious competitor. He loved to win, and he never turned that off—even when he wasn't playing or practicing. One day after practice he was on the field throwing a football around. We were at about the 50-yard line, and of course Lawrence had to create a situation that involved a bet. Now Lawrence was probably the greatest linebacker to ever play the game, but he believed there was nothing in sports, let alone football, that he couldn't do. He made a wager with me that he could throw a football 50 yards and hit the right upright of the goalpost.

If I heard that from John Elway, who had one of the best throwing arms in history, I would say, "No, you can't." I turned to Lawrence and said, "There is no way you can possibly do that."

For the next twenty minutes I stood there, along with some of my teammates, and watched Lawrence throw footballs at the goalpost—and not hit it once. We were keeping track of how much money he was losing with each miss.

Finally, I gave him one "free" throw where if he hit it he would break even and if he missed it, his tally wouldn't go up. He missed and we all went into the locker room. Lawrence was a man of his word. He reached in his pocket, grabbed a huge wad of cash, peeled off a few bills, and threw them on the floor.

"There," he said. "Go get it."

"It doesn't embarrass me to have to pick money up off the floor," I said, reaching down to collect my winnings.

Outside the locker room was a basketball rim, complete with a net and backboard. Every now and then Lawrence would say, "I'll make ten foul shots in a row for a hundred dollars." It was always something that would turn into a competition and then a wager. As he took off his socks he'd roll them up and say, "I'll bet you ten bucks I can throw them into the hamper across the room." Now every once in a while Lawrence would win one of these wagers, such as hitting the ten foul shots in a row because he was a very good basketball player.

There are many other players besides Jim Brown and Lawrence Taylor who legitimately deserve to be called great. One who played my position and came into the league the same year I did was Joe Montana. Joe was the first quarterback I know who played with a sense of nobility. He played with grace and style that gave you the impression that it was just so easy for him, that the name "Joe Cool" fit him perfectly.

Without question, he was playing the position differently than the rest of the quarterbacks in the NFL. A lot of it was talent, but also he was being taught by Bill Walsh, the master of quarterback fundamentals. I played in the league for fifteen years and have been broadcasting football for ten years. I have yet to come across another quarterback who was as graceful and smooth as Joe Montana was dropping back and throwing.

Darrell Green was, by far, my greatest nemesis. I never played against anyone else like him. He just could cover so well. Even when the receiver was open and you'd throw it, he'd still knock down the pass. He was unbelievably fast and his ability to change direction was phenomenal.

We played many a game against Washington where Bill said, "Simms, no matter what you do, I don't care what you read, don't you throw the football to Darrell Green's side."

"Okay, Coach, I got it," I'd say.

We would start the game and I would throw every pass to the opposite side of Darrell Green. I am not exaggerating— every single one. The Redskins were pretty smart. They decided to take the safety out of the middle of the field and use him to help double-cover the receiver to my left. As a quarterback I was trained, when the defense double-covers the receiver on your left, to throw to the receiver on the right, where there is single coverage. In this case the right happened to be Darrell's side.

One particular play I remember as if it were yesterday was an out cut I threw on second down. I delivered a great pass. I could see it coming out of my hand. Perfect spiral. Perfect speed. It was going to be right on target. At the last second I let out a gasp, because Darrell seemingly came out of nowhere to cut right in front of the receiver full speed. Anticipating the interception, I took off toward the sideline so that I would be in position to make the tackle before he reached the end zone. Darrell got both hands on the ball but couldn't quite hold on. The ball hit the ground. I let out a huge sigh.

As I turned to the sideline for the next play to be signaled in, Bill Parcells was 5 yards onto the field. His headset was on the ground. He was screaming at me at the top of his lungs.

"I told you not to throw to his side!"

"But, Bill, they're double-covering the receiver to my left," I yelled back.

"I don't care if they triple-cover him! Don't throw it any-where near Darrell Green!"

In all the times I played against Darrell—and it was twice a year for about ten seasons—he intercepted only one pass of mine because I'll bet I didn't throw five his way in all those years. If he covered a guy we'd basically wipe him off the play. That receiver was invisible. We would not throw to him. We threw it to the tight end or somebody else who was single-covered. Often when we would put three wide receivers out there, Darrell was so good, so nimble, that even if you beat him—unless you just whipped it in there quickly—he'd recover and still make a play on the football.

I only got to play against Michael Haynes, the Hall of Fame cornerback with the Patriots and Raiders, a couple of times. He was unbelievable, too. He just could completely shut a player out of the game. Once, playing against the Raiders, I threw a pass his way, about 15 to 20 yards downfield. Michael stepped in front of the receiver and got both hands on the ball as clean as could be, as if we were playing catch. Fortunately I threw a pretty hard ball, because it hit both of his hands, bounced up in the air, and my guy caught it.

Michael was different, because at six feet two he was taller and had more range than a lot of other corners. With his size he could engulf receivers, because there weren't that many big receivers when he played. Boy, next to most of them, he looked like a giant.

Besides tremendous physical skills, another thing that great players have in common is that they love and can't live without competition. And then they have the unique capacity to apply it to the playing field.

It's a lesson I constantly had to relearn in the off-season when I was with the Giants. Every year we would bring in different newcomers to the team—a linebacker, a wide receiver, a defensive back—and they would have exceptional physical skills. And I would think, *Man, have we found a hidden gem in the National Football League.*

Then we would go through minicamp, training camp, and preseason games. That's when we would find out that those players lacked the competitive desire to succeed or the capacity to apply their skills to the playing field—and one by one they would be released.

Today's NFL players are better conditioned than when I played, simply because of advances in nutrition and the modern science behind training. To give you an idea of what I'm talking about, when I entered the league, our weight-lifting program at Morehead State was far ahead of what the Giants or most other NFL teams were doing, even though we were basically working out in a big garage and the conditions were terrible.

At Morehead we had no machines and all of our free weights were home-made by the head coach. There weren't even any imprints with the weight totals on them. These were just slabs of steel. The only exercises we did in college were bench presses and pull-ups for the upper body, and dead lifts, squats, sit-ups, and toe-raisers for the lower body. We did a lot of sprinting, too.

But at the time, off-season conditioning and training had yet to fully evolve throughout the NFL. We did have a weight coach, but the conditioning program was not scientific. It wasn't planned from the start to the finish of the off-season as it is now. The approach was basically, "Do whatever you want to do."

Now it's so much better, so much more specific, so much smarter. It makes players more explosive and more durable. A lot of top players even have personal trainers. I never had one. I don't think I ever had a teammate on the Giants with a personal trainer. Back then the only athletes with personal trainers had four legs and dined on oats. However, today's players increase their chances of having longer careers because they take such good care of themselves.

If someone were to ask me what has been the biggest change in the game since I played, I think it's the extraordinary skill level of the wide receivers catching the football. Not only are they bigger and faster than ever, but they also can catch the ball anywhere, at any angle. Catches that would have accounted for the top highlight reel for a whole season ten years ago are what you get in a weekly package now.

We are seeing tremendous influxes of taller, more athletic players at the receiver position—including those among a record seven that entered the league as first-rounders in 2004. It used to be that you looked for a receiver who was five foot ten, who could run well and catch the ball. Now teams are looking for—

and finding—receivers who are at least six-one and can still run well and catch the ball.

Some of it is due to genetics and diet. Some of it is due to teams throwing the ball more at all levels of football. Some of it is due to the popularity of the NFL. The kid who grows up watching the games can see that wide receivers are making most of the big plays, so that's what they want to do. Either that, or those same athletes want to be the defensive backs that cover those receivers.

Heading into the draft, we used to talk about seven to ten running backs as possible first-round picks. Now it is hard finding one. In '04, only two running backs were number one picks, and both were late first-rounders at that—Oregon State's Steven Jackson, to St. Louis, and Virginia Tech's Kevin Jones, to Detroit. I also believe that kids know they have a better chance for success and a longer pro career as a wide receiver or a defensive back than as a running back.

There are a lot of ways to get the ball to the receiver. You see teams run reverses. They throw screens. They throw short passes. I've seen extremely talented wide receivers catch a lot of balls from what I consider very average quarterbacks because coaches will find a way to take advantage of those wonderful pass-catching skills. They also want to do whatever they can to exploit the officials' new emphasis on enforcing the rule that prohibits contact with a receiver beyond five yards of the line of scrimmage.

Offenses spread the field with three, four and even five wide receivers because they know if they don't they're not going to have any success. Athletes on defense are just too good to give them the advantage of covering only a small area. You have to make the opponent defend as much of the field as possible. Where would you have a better chance of getting open? In a space that is six-by-ten or a space that is twenty-by-twenty?

Ron Erhardt recognized earlier than most coaches the advantages of spreading the field with formations. We were one of the first teams in the NFL to send the back out of the backfield and get that three–wide receiver look. I thought that was some really wild stuff. I thought we were wide open. Now when teams introduce their starting lineup, they introduce three wide receivers sometimes. If they're the best players on your team, why use a fullback who can block a guy every once in a while as opposed to a third receiver who can make a larger contribution?

Mike Martz had long before arrived at that conclusion as offensive coordinator with St. Louis, especially in Kurt Warner's first year there. He knew his best chance for success was to spread the field with what at the time was probably the fastest group of receivers in the league. What made that approach even more difficult for opposing defenses to handle was Martz's play calling, which was both innovative and extremely aggressive.

Spreading the field also became the best answer that offensive coaches could find to what once had been the bane of their existence—the "46" (aka "Bear") defense that Buddy Ryan introduced while he was defensive coordinator of the Chicago Bears from the late '70s to mid-'80s. It had a lot to do with helping the Bears win Super Bowl XX.

What made that defense so unique was that the safeties and linebackers were lined up in positions different from those you were used to seeing. You expect to see safeties in the back of the defense. Now all of a sudden you've got a safety lining up 2 yards from the center, almost right in front of you. As a quarterback you're thinking, *What is this? Oh, that's a safety?* In fact, the scheme got its name from the jersey number of one of the Bears' hardest-hitting and most disruptive safeties at the time, Doug Plank.

You also expect to see linebackers spread out evenly across the line of scrimmage. Now all of a sudden you have two line-backers, within a yard of each other, at one end of the line.

The best comparison would be to spend all your life count-ing one, two, three, four, five, six, seven, eight, nine, ten, and then all of a sudden being told, "Okay, for this week, we want you to count three, one, two, seven, six, five, nine, eight, ten." It truly was that confusing.

Dave Duerson, another of the Bears' safeties, tried to add to that confusion and maybe create a distraction by coming up around the center and barking like a dog. I wondered, *Is this sup-posed to scare me?* I'm not sure how much he actually distracted me, but it was really strange and kind of funny. I will say this about Dave: he was a very good barker; he really did sound like a dog.

But confusion wasn't the only problem the "46" defense posed. It wasn't even the biggest. The biggest problem was that you were forced to block the most talented defensive lineman one-on-one because you had to account for the other pass rush-ers around him. With Chicago, Richard Dent often was that guy. When Buddy Ryan became head coach in Philadelphia, he did the same thing with Reggie White. In both cases, that would almost always create a mismatch.

Other factors that made the "Bear" defense such a headache for the offense—and especially for the quarterback—were that you didn't practice against it on a regular basis and it wasn't something you saw other teams use. We actually devoted a whole week in training camp before the 1985 season to working against it—and the Bears weren't even on our schedule. We did that mainly because we thought we would be in the playoffs that year and might end up facing Chicago, but our coaches also wanted us to be prepared just in case any other teams tried to duplicate that defense.

Sure enough, we did face the Bears in the second round of the postseason. We lost, 21-0, so the extra work against the "46" didn't pay off as we had hoped. But as physically talented as the Bears were, they could have lined up in a base defense that we saw every week and probably still kicked our butt. Then, when you take those very talented players and put them in a unique scheme, you usually get greatness, which was what Chicago's defense achieved that season.

The rest of the league began studying Buddy Ryan's "46" closely, and one day an offensive coordinator somewhere finally said, "If you spread them out, what do they do then?" As more and more offenses went to three and four wide receivers and expanded the field, it did create tremendous problems for the Bears. You had linebackers out in space against wide receivers, and no matter how good a linebacker you are, you cannot cover wide receivers like that.

Not that that killed the "46" altogether. The scheme still had some effective components, and for each one that offensive coordinators tried to take away there were others that defensive coordinators salvaged by making different alterations. Even today you see many derivatives of the "46." I still see it in almost every game from almost every team. Sometimes it's hard to recognize because offenses have so many formations, but you know you're looking at it when you see the center and both guards facemask-to-facemask with three defensive linemen.

In general, when you see that alignment in the NFL, it usually means the other team is going to blitz you. The idea is to make the two guards and center block those three defensive linemen, while bringing either a safety or a linebacker from the outside so that the tackles have to block them as the three guys work one-on-one on the inside. And if one of those defensive linemen is especially talented, then the one-on-one is actually a mismatch and the guards can't get any help from the tackles.

Take any team in the National Football League and you can figure out which receivers, based on talent level, will have the ball in their hands more than the others. That includes pass-catching running backs such as Marshall Faulk and Priest Holmes. Number them from one to four or five, and I promise you—barring injuries—when the season's up, the catches will reflect that order because you're always going to work harder to get the ball in the hands of the guys who can really do something with it.

All the players know that order, too. They know where they stand. During our production meetings I've had receivers tell me, "Come on, I'm the third option. You know it and I know it. I'm going to be the third option on every play."

"You're absolutely right," I'll say. "But you'd better be ready because when they do come to you, that's your chance, so you'd better be open."

As Don Coryell would always say with that trademark lisp of

his, "Let's get the ball to the guy who can score touchdowns." And it is that simple: Give it to the people who can make plays. You don't hand the ball twenty times a game to your fullback. You hand it to that halfback because he's the game breaker. Why did Terrell Owens always catch a lot more passes than the guy who was on the other side of the field playing wide receiver for the 49ers? Because he was the best receiver.

Someone once said to me, "The Giants always knew how to get the ball to the tight end."

"What do you mean?" I said.

"Well, Mark Bavaro and Zeke Mowatt caught a lot of passes."

"Yeah, they caught a lot of passes because they were our best receivers."

And because they were our best receivers we designed plays for them. We put them in formations. We moved them. We split them out. We put them at tight end. We ran them down the field. We ran them short. We did just about everything we could with them in the passing game.

If the tight end is not of that caliber, then you change formations, you move players around, and you get a wide receiver in the tight end position and he runs the tight-end routes. That's what all teams do. The plays they run are exactly the same, regardless of who they have running the pass routes. Instead of the fullback running into the flat, they send the tight end into the flat. If they put in a wide receiver where the tight end would usually go, that's because that wide receiver is better than the tight end.

• • •

Coaching has gotten better in all terms. Coaches are much better at technical instruction and they study the game much more. Consider this routine that Tom Moore, offensive coordinator of the Indianapolis Colts, told me he follows the day before a home game: He takes his wife to lunch, drops her off at home, goes to the team hotel at 1:30 to 2 o'clock, turns on the TV to college football, turns down the sound, and spends the rest of the afternoon pacing and calling the plays he is going to call on Sunday. He reads his sheets, goes over his notes, and gets thoroughly prepared for the game.

Coaches are, without question, more willing to take chances than when I played. A lot of that simply correlates to the same type of thinking that exists throughout society. Weren't we living a more conservative lifestyle ten or fifteen years ago? Think about how far we've come in technology the last ten years in the American way of life. Everybody has computers and cell phones and all sorts of wireless devices (after many years of resistance, even I use e-mail and have a cell phone). Football's the same way. Either keep moving or lose.

Offensive coaches will throw the ball in situations where you'd normally expect to see a run. As a result defensive coaches are more willing to blitz because even though it can sometimes be risky, you have to take that chance to match the higher level of talent among quarterbacks and receivers, as well as the aggressive passing you see week in and week out.

It is all about play calling. Not which plays you call but when you call them. I'll go as far as to say that nothing determines the success or failure of the offense more than the play-calling sequence. Give two offenses the same talent at every position, the same playbooks but different people calling the plays, chances are they will have different results.

For instance, if Team A runs the ball on every first and second down and only throws in obvious passing situations, it will not have a great chance to be productive on a consistent level, because most defenses will be able to anticipate those calls. On the other hand, if Team B runs play-action passes, reverses, and an occasional flea-flicker or trick play on first down, it will force the defense to guess and become less aggressive—thus allowing for greater offensive success. You answer the questions of which plays to call through study during the week, but on Sunday do you have the courage to call certain plays at the right time—when you think the defense won't be ready for them—and not worry about the consequences?

Unconventional plays work because the routine, mundane plays also work, and defenses try too hard to counter them. You run off tackle three times in a row, at 4 yards a crack, and then the defense says, "We're going to stop the run off right tackle." But the next time, instead of running off right tackle, you fake it and run a reverse. The backside guy that's supposed to look for the reverse is tired of looking for it and not seeing it. He just wants to tackle the runner, so he's now out of position to stop the end who has come around and taken the ball, and that's why the reverse works.

Play calling is an art. A lot of coaches in the NFL can design plays that are sound and that give their players a chance to have success. But they just don't have the feel for when to call those plays at the proper time in a game. It's like Paul Newman said to Jackie Gleason just before their big showdown game of pool at the end of the movie *The Hustler:* "Fast and loose, fat man! That's what you're going to get."

That same philosophy applies to offensive coordinators in today's game. The good ones call plays without fear. They trust what all of their film study has shown them. They trust their instincts. And they don't second-guess themselves.

Mike Martz certainly takes that approach. If it were up to him, the St. Louis Rams would just be pedal to the metal at all times. You can almost hear him saying before a game, "I've got a hundred new plays, and let's get them all in today." But there are consequences with that philosophy. When you go pedal to the metal, the quarterback gets beat up, then he becomes inconsistent, and then everybody starts lacking confidence in him.

I'm not saying Mike is always right, but I know this: There's not a current or former quarterback who doesn't want to play for him for at least a year or two and say, "Let's go, Coach. Rip it!" Quarterbacks are all alike. We can't throw it enough. You know, maybe deep down, it's not the thing to do for the overall good of the team sometimes, but who cares? You're having fun while you're doing it.

But the fact is, in the NFL, nobody gets a free pass. Mike might get the free pass calling the plays, but somebody's going to end up suffering. Too many hits on the quarterback. Too many big hits on the receivers. You're putting your defense at risk because by throwing so much, you prolong the game and give the other team a couple of more possessions. Anytime you do something on one side of the ball, there are always ramifications on the other side.

Nobody operates in a vacuum in this game, least of all the

coach calling the plays. He is under constant pressure not only to make the right decisions but also to be a good time manager. From the moment the whistle blows to end one play, he has all of forty seconds to figure out what he wants to call . . . and communicate it through his headset down to the sidelines while allowing enough time for that coach to relay the play to the transmitter in the quarterback's helmet . . . and for the quarterback to share it with the rest of the players in the huddle, get to the line of scrimmage, change the play if needed, call out the signals . . . and take the snap before the play clock shows zeros.

Sometimes as he comes to the line the quarterback has to hesitate for a second to allow the blocking calls to be made. There is a whole language that offensive linemen, backs, and tight ends have to tell each other: "You're going to pull. . . . You're going to be blocking down. . . . I'll block your guy; you block mine." Of course, they can't make those calls until they get down in their stance and see what the defense is going to do—which is yet another factor that the play caller must keep in mind.

When I was hurt during the 1992 season, I spent one game sitting in the booth with Jim Fassel, the Giants' offensive coordinator at the time, as he called the plays. I couldn't believe how fast he had to think. He would call the play but he wouldn't even look up because he would be going over all the scenarios of what was coming next. Just before the snap he would look up, watch the play, then immediately put his head down and say, "Okay, what is it? Third-and-seven? Let's go with this."

Jim spent 90 percent of his time looking at his play sheet

during the game. I couldn't even watch the game because I was so focused on watching him work the play sheet. I was just shocked at how fast it all happened for him. In his decision making, he literally had a window of about three to five seconds, max, to make a decision.

On the field, on the receiving end, it was just the opposite. I'd be saying, "What's taking so long? Give me the play. What's so hard? Just call the play and let's go!" I had never played the game from the coordinator's perspective. Watching Jim gave me a tremendous appreciation for it.

Until you walk a mile in the other man's Nikes, you never know how rough it is.

CHAPTER NINE

The Next Generation

For the most part I like the league that my son Christopher has entered as a young quarterback. The only drawback I see is that there is a lot less patience among fans and media than there was when I played. Coaches are less patient, too, because they know, with salary-cap constraints and free agency causing rampant player movement each year, there is no such thing as a building process.

Owners listen to the criticism from fans and media. They also see the success other teams are having and want the same for their clubs. They saw the Baltimore Ravens go from nowhere to win the Super Bowl. They saw the New England Patriots go from nowhere to win two Super Bowls in three seasons. Don't we all say: Why not us? Why him and not me?

There's just a greater chance of ups and downs than there used to be because you can't keep things in place. Why does Drew Bledsoe have an explosive offense one year in Buffalo and then, the following season, the Bills are trying to be a running, ball-control team? Because they lose a wide receiver, Peerless Price, and a tight end, Jay Riemersma, to free agency in the off-season. That was absolutely unheard of when I played.

When you have greater stability and continuity, you can play at a more even keel than you can now. You don't see the dramatic changes in win-loss records of teams that you have now. You don't see quarterbacks' statistics change as much as they do now, either.

The game is good. Really good. Could it be better? Yes. I'd like to see more stability with the rosters in the league. Just a little. I still want movement so that players can get their money, and I like the competition we have with all the teams. But I'd like to see a little more separation—teams that can pull away from the pack because they are better and because they've been able to keep together a group of players long enough to let them progress and develop with the same coach. I'd like to see it go back to a more pure form where the good work of coaches and talent evaluators pays the greatest dividends rather than how clever your "capologist" can be with a calculator.

You could be a great X-and-O coach and a great evaluator of talent, but because of the salary cap, you can't keep that talent to allow it to progress.

Generally, I think quarterbacks are better able to come into the league and mentally get up to speed faster than ever. Talent is one reason, of course. But other big reasons are that they're used to playing in the spotlight, because they receive more publicity in high school and in college. They're used to playing in systems that throw the ball much more and—through coaching and the more sophisticated defenses they face—they have to think much harder at the college level than ever before. And that just makes them a more polished product when they come into the NFL.

Peyton Manning, Daunte Culpepper, and Donovan McNabb are three top-notch, kick-ass young quarterbacks. I consider them the core of players in the league at the position. These are guys who have done it for quite a few years now, yet they're still young. Overall, I like the quality of the young quarterbacks in the NFL, but I feel sorry for them, too, because they're not given the chance to develop sometimes as I think they can because of the impatience of teams, the fans, and the media.

I don't like the instability of the current quarterbacking climate for my son's sake, but I've never once said or thought, *God, I wish he never would have played football.* Even with all that instability, with all the criticism and all those negative forces a quarterback has to deal with on the outside and even on the inside, I don't have the slightest reservations about Christopher playing in the NFL.

Actually, the criticism is a lot of the reason you're in the game. You like that feeling of wondering, *How's it going to turn out today? Are we going to fall off that tightrope or are we going to survive for another day?* I never wonder if that will be too much for my son to handle. If Christopher didn't like it I don't think he would have progressed as far as he has. He would have decided to give it up in high school, or I would have seen the passion leave him.

Playing should be fun at all levels, but that is particularly important—maybe even crucial—when you're a kid. When I played quarterback for the sixth-grade football team at St. Rita's School in Louisville, it was so much fun. We did win. We had success. But we also had so much fun.

We'd come to practice, and at least one night a week the coach would have us choose up sides and play backyard football the whole time. You'd laugh with snot coming out of your nose, it was such a good time. We had a little equipment and there was a little organization. There were some nights that we actually went through some regimented drills and did handoffs and form tackling, and there were games, of course. But it was just all about fun. I couldn't wait to go to practice.

Then, in seventh grade, it changed. There were new coaches. There was new teaching, a new way of doing things, and I thought, *This is really a drag.* I didn't like it. It just wasn't what I wanted it to be. It was way too serious. The approach went from being fun to just being so serious.

After a couple of games I didn't go to practice one night. I just said, "I don't even want to go." My dad said, "Hey, look, boy, if you don't like it, then don't play. It's just that simple. Only play sports because you like to do it. Don't do it because you think we want you to." I quit football for the rest of the year.

In eighth grade I decided I wanted to play again. I thought maybe it would be different because I was older and maybe changed my outlook somewhat. It was a little better, but it still wasn't what I wanted. We had some success and I enjoyed it, but I was still looking for that first experience.

Your first experience in organized sports is so meaningful because it truly can go one way or the other as far as your entire outlook on playing as you get older, especially organized football. Even youth football is complicated because you've still got to get the players orchestrated enough to make it all work. But you've still got to have fun, because you're dealing with kids.

Coaches have so much to do with making it right, and that applies to any level. When my younger son, Matthew, was nine years old I started coaching his baseball team. From the very start I set the parameters for the players and the parents: "Let's make sure we do this the right way. Let's make sure all the kids play. And let's have fun. We'll still try to be competitive, but we'll have fun."

It worked pretty well. I only got a couple of complaints because there were a couple of kids who weren't going to play as much as the other ones, but they still played. Looking back, I'm pretty happy with what we tried to accomplish because we did have a good time.

Even though Bill Parcells was a hard-driving, hard-core guy, there was something about the way he did things that still made it special, still made it fun. There was something in there that kept us feeling like kids. For instance, he liked to make us compete against one another in practice, which always made for a good time. That's why you play—because you love to compete. And competing during the week, in addition to Sunday, was a great way to help maintain your enthusiasm and focus through what otherwise could become a dreary routine. Competing and having fun are what keep you playing this game. If it were all just serious hard work without any joy or love for the game, if it were all just about collecting a paycheck, why would you play?

Early in Christopher's life, I thought it might be a little more of a challenge for him to have fun on the field because he always has been subjected to more scrutiny than other kids playing football. When your father plays quarterback in the NFL, it just goes with the territory. You're judged differently, no matter what sport you play.

It began happening as soon as Christopher started playing sports—fourth grade, fifth grade. People knew who his dad was, and they would make sure that he knew that they knew. He'd go walking by the other team, getting ready to play basketball, and hear sarcastic comments like, "There he is. . . . There's the Simms kid. . . ." I was not that upset about it. I don't know that I anticipated it, but in a sad way, I just understand human nature. That's just the way it is when you have a recognizable name. You want to beat those kinds of people. It's similar to football players who love to beat the defending Super Bowl champion. I guess, deep down, it's not meant to be personal. It's just the competitive nature of people.

I never felt I had to say much to Christopher about it. He seemed to grasp it at a fairly young age, so it was a subject we didn't have to talk much about. I felt assured that he knew what was going on and he seemed to handle it. If he wouldn't have handled it well, I think I would have spoken up.

It also tapped into his competitive juices. He knew what he

had to do to silence his critics, and that was to play well. Some of my favorite moments playing in the National Football League were when I walked out of the visitors' locker room to the field and heard the fans cursing and yelling at me. There is nothing like people rooting against you when you play. It just makes winning better and you just like the atmosphere of the competition. And I would think, in a similar fashion, that was how it felt to Christopher, too.

When I was growing up, I don't remember one kid ever saying he wanted to be a professional athlete. I don't even remember any kid I grew up with who even talked about playing college baseball, football or anything. People didn't even talk about my playing college football until the end of my junior year of high school. Now if you go to a Little League baseball game, every single one of those kids wants to and thinks he's going to be a major league player. It's just more prevalent. It's just more talked about.

I try to guard against sounding like another one of those parents who talk about their children playing professional sports someday, but when Christopher was young, yeah, I knew he could throw the ball well and would have a chance to be a pro. Because I was still playing for the Giants I got to see him play only two youth football games in my life, but the throwing ability was easy to see. By the time he was about ten, playing in a recreational league, I said, "Oh, boy, he can really throw it."

I went to watch him play a game when he was in seventh grade and I was actually enjoying it because he was getting to throw quite a bit. I said to myself, *Wow! He's getting to throw it more than I do in game.* But the opponent was good, and at one point Christopher took a hard hit. It stunned him a little. As he was lying on the ground, the other team's players, coaches, parents and other fans couldn't have been happier or more excited. They were screaming. They were yelling.

I knew Christopher was going to be okay. He sat up. He stood up. He shook it off. He kept playing. Was I surprised by the reaction of the opposing team and its fans? Yes, I was a little surprised. I guess people just can't always help themselves. We're all competitive. We all take a certain bit of satisfaction in doing something better than someone else, and maybe it's a little more satisfying when you can say—in whatever form it comes—that you got the best of a professional athlete.

When Christopher started to play at Ramapo, New Jersey, High School, as a freshman, I realized he was an exceptional thrower. It's like watching a bunch of kids run and always being able to pick out the fastest. I could easily pick out the kid who could throw it better than the other kids, and it was usually my son.

Other people could see it, too. Along with his last name it became something that people from opposing schools could focus on in a derisive way. One time in particular was when Ramapo played on the road and Christopher threw an incompletion deep down the field. The public-address announcer for the other team, with as much sarcasm as he could, said, "Whoa! That pass by Simms traveled fifty-three yards in the air. . . . Incomplete!"

But there were advantages to his growing up the son of an NFL quarterback. I could take him out in the backyard and show him how to throw—the little, technical points to help refine his mechanics. I probably told him a few things in high school that another father couldn't have told his son, such as how to recognize a blitz. During his sophomore year he would bring the game film home on Mondays and we would watch it together. One day I pointed out that when he saw that the safety was somewhere other than the middle or lined up tight to the line, a blitz was coming.

"Oh, wow!" Christopher said. "I didn't know that."

After that, whenever he saw teams were going to blitz, he'd make a call—I think it was "Black Eighty"—that told the line the defense was blitzing, and the tight end and backs to stay in. One receiver would run an in-cut, the other would run a post. Christopher would just pick the one that was open and throw it.

It's the same with my other son, Matthew, a quarterback at Don Bosco Prep in Ramsey, New Jersey. When he was in eighth grade I went to some of his practices, and one day his coach asked me, "Is there anything you want to put in our offense?"

I taught Matthew and the rest of the team about "Over and Under," which means there's a receiver deep and a receiver short—two guys basically running the same pattern, or mirroring each other, at different depths, such as 5 yards and 20 yards.

Being in the eighth grade, Matthew knew only one thing when he dropped back to pass: "If there's a receiver at 20 yards, I'm throwing it to him."

"Okay, Matt," I told him. "But there are two defenders covering that guy. When there are two defenders on him, that means nobody's covering the receiver underneath, at five yards. Throw it to him."

"But that's only five yards. I want to throw it down the field."

"Yeah, but if you throw it down the field, there's a good chance one of those defenders will knock it down or intercept you. If you throw it to the guy at five yards, he'll catch it and run for twenty."

After many incomplete passes and interceptions in practice, Matthew finally caught on to the idea of throwing it to the guys who are not covered.

I can't say that I taught Christopher much of anything when he was at the University of Texas because I wasn't there. It was up to his coaches to do that. Would I like to have been there to work with him? Sure. What father wouldn't? But it wasn't possible.

Over the last ten years or so I've worked with about a hundred high school and college quarterbacks. I do about fifty sessions a year at any available field near my home. Most of the kids come from New Jersey. They are sons of my friends or sons of friends of my friends, or quarterbacks who play for coaches I know. I always like their fathers or coaches to accompany them so that they can absorb the information along with the quarterback and help reinforce it later.

I don't get compensated for this. I just enjoy doing it and I know it means a lot to the kids and to their parents and coaches. To watch these young quarterbacks throw a football and do it right and give you that knowing smile when they do is an unbelievable feeling for both of us.

I'm proud of it. I'm not saying there's any one way to teach. I know a way. I also know that every time I work with a kid I can improve him in a day. Not a week. Not a month. One day. I guarantee that when he leaves me he will see a dramatic difference in what he's doing.

I've taught the kids so much that I've retaught myself a lot of fundamentals as well. I always throw footballs during these sessions to demonstrate how I want it done. But I will admit, each year I'm not throwing quite as hard or quite as far, and, yes, my arm is starting to get a little bit sore sooner than it used to. Those are just certain realities that come with age.

The most time I ever spent working with my oldest son was after he got out of college, in preparing for the scouting combine in February and for his pre-draft workouts. We probably threw and did more stuff at that point than at any other time in our lives because there were no classes for him to attend, he wasn't involved in any drills at Texas, and my NFL broadcasting season was over. So we were able to just go outside and throw.

My son has two qualities that I like in a quarterback: endurance and a strong arm. So when we did practice it was never for less than two hours at a time. During that span he easily threw two to three hundred passes, and his arm never wore out. He has big hands, long arms, and a very strong throwing arm, all of which have a lot to do with his ability to throw a football for as long as he wants. But I think a lot of it is simply that he likes to practice. He likes to throw. He does it a lot, and when you do a lot of throwing, you become conditioned to take it physically. You don't get tired easily.

My younger son, Matthew, did the first extensive throwing of his life in the summer of 2003, just before his freshman year of high school. The first couple of weeks his arm would get sore after throwing. You get sore because your throwing mechanics are not right and your body is not conditioned to handle the workload. When something is not in sequence, it's rougher on the body, it puts more strain on it, and that's what creates soreness. As time has gone on, Matthew has reached the point where he can throw for long periods of time and his arm never gets sore.

I cover everything in my workouts with young quarterbacks. The first thing, always, is I want the drop to be perfect because that sets up everything else. What is a perfect drop? Simply put, it is no wasted steps, good rhythm, proper weight balance, and when the drop is finished, finding yourself in the correct position to throw the football. As I always tell them, "We're starting a race. If you get a bad start, it's hard to make up ground. Let's not do that."

You work on getting into the right position to make all the throws—and there are a lot of them. If you get in the right position it usually works out well. We're talking about shoulder placement and foot placement, two very key components that will help make you a consistent thrower.

The reality of throwing is just like golf. You think you're doing something right and you're not. What you perceive you look like and what it feels like are always two different things. The best teaching tool is the video camera, which I used during those sessions with Christopher. That way, when you tell a quarterback his shoulder is out of line and that's why he threw it poorly, and he says, "Oh, no, it is in line," you can show him the reality on the tape.

When you work on techniques it becomes a feel. You feel right and you feel wrong. Regardless of the student, once you teach him the basic principles of what you're trying to do, you keep working on them until all of a sudden he starts to get the physical sense of right and wrong. When he does it wrong he knows it immediately. He can feel it in his own body that it wasn't as rhythmic or as easy as it should have been.

Why do you become good at something? Because you repeat what you do time and time again. That's how you get good. That's why it takes tremendous practice time. I tell kids all the time, "If you want to get good at throwing, you have to throw a lot. A lot!"

You're talking about putting a large object in your hand and trying to throw it 20, 30, and sometimes 40 yards down the field. You're talking about trying to put the ball through a very small space. There are many technical aspects of this that must be done right in order to have success, and technical improvement comes only through repetition.

Take the best foul-shooters in NBA history: Larry Bird, Calvin Murphy, Rick Barry. I know they had natural-born talent, but they made themselves the best through incredible amounts of work at making their fundamentals perfect and countless hours of shooting free throws. They did it so much that regardless of the situation or the elements, when they stepped to that line, they just put the ball through the net. It was automatic. It was robotic. They were like machines.

The same is true for a quarterback. When you're good, you reach a point where you don't think about anything. You do it naturally. Then you watch films of the game, your coach points out that you did so many things technically right, and it doesn't even register with you. The reason you did those things right had nothing to do with what happened on Sunday. It was the result of what took place during all of those days, weeks, months, and years of training.

After a while, that constant practice just becomes part of you.

There is a certain amount of nervousness that all parents feel when they watch their children in athletic competition. It is the fear of the unknown. Will they perform at a level that makes them happy and makes us feel good because they're happy? And if it doesn't go well for your son or daughter, what are you going to say to help them feel better about it? Let's be realistic here. Regardless of your child's athletic ability, there are going to be a lot of rough moments.

When my oldest son was playing football in high school and college, usually a day or two before his game I would call him from whatever city I was in for an NFL telecast. I would give him reminders about some physical aspects of the game—such as making sure he warmed up properly and that his drops were good and to use his snap count to try and draw the other team offside—and just talk about football in general.

"Remember, it's not always going to go well," I'd say. "There could be some bad times, and if you go through them, just forget them—move on and remain positive. Whatever happens in your mind, your body will respond accordingly. If you think positive, your body will react that way, too." I'd like to take full credit for those words, but I can't. Bill Parcells said them to me any number of times. Good advice is worth passing along.

Now my son is in the pros. We still talk at least once a week during the season, and those conversations have changed dramatically. The first game he ever played with the Buccaneers was in the 2003 preseason opener against the Jets in Tokyo. We spoke two days before the game and I asked him, "How was the trip? How do you like Japan?"

I was about ready to give him the usual football pointers, but I suddenly stopped myself. Once my son signed that NFL contract it was pretty much over in terms of my giving him that kind of football advice.

"Well, son," I said with a laugh, "I guess there's nothing I can really go over with you because I know Jon Gruden and his staff have covered everything."

Christopher started laughing.

"Dad, you are right," he said. "They have gone over every possible scenario you can think of."

And after all the games he had played, I have to say that the most relaxed I have ever been watching my son in action was when I got up at five o'clock in the morning Eastern Time to watch that first preseason game in Tokyo live on ESPN. I knew that he'd be prepared. I just knew he belonged there. I had the same feeling the first time I saw him play a game in high school and in college. I could see that, physically, at least he was on a par with the rest of the players on the field.

My son has gone out in the world and it's no different for me than for other parents I know who have sent their sons or daughters to New York City to work for the first time. They're on their own. We try to watch. We still worry about them because they're our children. They're going to make mistakes. They're going to experience all that life has to offer, good and bad.

Whenever I watch Christopher play on television I don't want anyone else around me except my family—Diana, Matthew, and my daughter, Deirdre. This tradition goes back to when he was at Texas. First of all, no one could possibly be more of a fan of my son than the people closest to him. Secondly, we are just much more comfortable in a setting that doesn't invite other points of view about Christopher's performance. We want to try and enjoy it as much as we can without any outside forces, and that includes turning down the sound.

Even though it's what I do for a living, I don't want another announcer telling me what my son is doing right or wrong as he plays. That is something I can recognize on my own. For that matter, Archie Manning probably turns down the sound whenever he watches us broadcast the games of his son, Peyton. I hope he doesn't, but I understand where he is coming from.

For the rest of the audience, I want them to listen because I am trying to give them the reasons why their team is winning or losing. I'm also going to give them a lot of information about why certain players are playing well and why certain players are not.

I understand why what we say as announcers sometimes drives people absolutely crazy. Occasionally I have my own frustrations with some of my colleagues who do NFL and college games, and, yes, that volume control can be your best defense. But it's even better to tune in to a broadcast that gives you the most accurate picture possible of what is happening on the field. That's what viewers should expect and demand.

And you never forget the people in your audience. Just as

when the Simms family gathers around the TV to watch their favorite NFL quarterback, there are all kinds of parents, grand-parents, siblings, and other relatives and friends hanging on every word they hear. When you talk about people in the huge forum that we have, you affect lives. You can't be careless with your comments during a broadcast. When I say that something is someone's fault or when I'm giving a compliment, I want to make sure that I am correct. I want to be truthful. I don't want to guess.

It takes work to make sure you are painting the proper per-spective of what is going on. I don't want to suggest that I am the only one in this business who invests the time and energy to find and dispense the truth, but I do try. And that's all you can really do.

ACKNOWLEDGMENTS

We **wish to thank** the following for their help in putting this book together:

Mauro DiPreta, whose skillful editing, great vision, and unwavering dedication to produce the very best book possible make him an All-Pro in his profession; Susan Weinberg and Cathy Hemming, for believing in the concept and for sharing great ideas for the framework; Joelle Yudin, for always being there to assist in every aspect of the production and to help keep things moving along; Steve Rosner, whose guidance and assistance were invaluable; and Basil Kane, a giant among literary agents.

We also would like to express our gratitude to Pat Hanlon, Erin Casey, Kirk Reynolds, Jack Brennan; Diana, Christopher, Deirdre, and Matthew Simms; Rhonda, Kristen, and Lindsay Carucci.

Phil Simms
FRANKLIN LAKES, NEW JERSEY

Vic Carucci
EAST AMHERST, NEW YORK